JAMES BRINDLEY

The First Canal Builder

JAMES BRINDLEY

THE FIRST CANAL BUILDER

NICK CORBLE

To Annette, for everything.

First published in 2005

Reprinted in 2011, 2014

The History Press
The Mill, Brimscombe Port,
Stroud, Gloucestershire, GL5 2QG
www.thehistorypress.co.uk

British Library Cataloguing in Publication Data.
A catalogue record for this book is available from the British Library.

ISBN 978 0 7524 3259 5

Printed in Great Britain by TJ International Ltd, Padstow, Cornwall

Contents

Introduction

Some had come to see a disaster, others simply for a spectacle, but what they in fact witnessed was the beginning of a revolution. All social strata were represented on the banks of the River Irwell just outside Manchester on that bright morning in July 1761, from the Earl of Stafford down to the humblest farmworker; and all were anticipating a show. The atmosphere amongst them was festive. Bunting decorated the few barges bobbing gently upon the water and a frisson of anticipation sharpened the mood.

A phalanx of stalls had appeared overnight, one of which was offering some kind of roasted meat. As the day settled, occasional gusts of wind started to spread smoke from the fires into the crowd, exciting the taste buds of those who hadn't tasted meat since the previous Sunday, as well as their superiors, most of whom had breakfasted off bacon and fish that morning. Everyone began to wonder if the day's events would be over in time for lunch.

There was no set schedule for those events, no printed handbill or official start time. In fact few of those present really knew what to expect. Most were simply enjoying the break from routine and the opportunity to be part of something different. Indeed, it wasn't long before a question mark began to hang over whether anything was going to happen at all. It seemed that the man whose ingenuity and reputation had drawn them all to the river that morning had disappeared.

One man, one common man, who, some said, had managed to trick a peer of the realm into staking his entire fortune on a venture the like of which had never been seen before and most thought preposterous. This venture, this notion, defied all reasonable expectation and even nature itself. One man, a very singular man, insisted everything would be alright. This was to be his moment of truth, but the word beginning to spread amongst the crowd was that he had retired to his bed.

Once sown, this rumour spread quickly, as if it had hitched a ride on the smoke from the fires. As it did so, wry smiles began to spread across the faces of some of the more colourfully and finely dressed of the assembly. Quite reasonably, they began to wonder if rather than coming to witness a challenge to the natural order of things they'd in fact come to see its reaffirmation. This

At the time of its building Brindley's aqueduct would have stood out as a marvel of construction in a largely rural setting. (Courtesy of The Waterways Archive)

lowly born upstart was to have his comeuppance it seemed. Speeches laced with homage were rapidly being rewritten, with an emphasis on sympathy laced with *schadenfreude*.

Others, more likely to be dressed in browns and greys, felt the first stirrings of disappointment. Many had come to believe in this man whose exploits in the last few months had earned him the nickname 'The Schemer'. They had already seen him perform marvels and they had begun to wonder if he might, just might, be about to deliver a miracle. They had bought into his dream of a new way of doing things and many had broken their backs for him making that dream a reality. More to the point, many of those looking for this miracle to happen were still owed wages.

By the end of the day everyone in the crowd would have their opinions and prejudices thoroughly tested, and debate on the merits of the missing man would be vociferous in the local inns. When they did finally get to eat that day, some sampled the sweet taste of success whilst others tucked into unseasoned slices of humble pie.

The man they would be talking about was James Brindley, the barely literate oldest son of an insignificant Staffordshire crofter; to some a mere millwright, to others an inspiration. We don't know for certain if Brindley did actually witness the events of that day, but his physical presence turned out to be immaterial. What we do know is that what followed turned out to be a decisive turning point in his life and career, setting in train a sequence of events that was both to make him and, in a relatively short space of time, break him.

But all this was to come. Where might Brindley have been as the stallholders pitched their stakes and the dignitaries gathered on the platform erected especially for the occasion? It is entirely likely that the rumours were true and he had retired to his bed, a habit he often adopted at moments of stress in his life. It's not unreasonable to suspect that Brindley had appreciated the importance of the day and succumbed to an attack of nerves. He was also not immune to bouts of self-doubt, even if these were usually short lived.

A quiet man at the best of times, crowds were not his natural milieu. He had tasted failure a few times in his career, seeing it as a natural part of the learning process, but never had he done so before a specially invited audience of the regional great and good of early Georgian society. However confident he may have been in success, even the faintest prospect of such a public failure was perhaps something best avoided. Equally, his natural introversion may have led him to reject the spotlight in favour of watching events unfold from the sidelines amongst the comfort of his men, observing with a critical eye rather than merely sightseeing.

When the show did finally get underway that warm July morning it took only minutes before Brindley's vision was vindicated and triumph was formally declared, but the crowds lingered for hours, unable it seemed to believe what their eyes had told them, before dispersing along with the last of the daylight. They were only the beginning. Others followed, and over the coming weeks tens of thousands would come and gaze and wonder at the structure before them, transforming the reputation of the man whose inspiration had made it all possible. From a moderately successful local figure, respected as someone who had hauled himself up from very little simply by dint of his skill and inventiveness, he would become a national guru in a whole new field of technology.

Before the year was out the process would begin that, in time, would cement his claim to be the country's first civil engineering superstar and the progenitor of a new transport system that was to transform the physical, social and economic landscape of the nation. Over the next dozen years he would work tirelessly as the great and good of the newly emerging industrial centres paid homage to his expertise until he eventually died, exhausted by a combination of overwork and undiagnosed diabetes.

Others, often his personal disciples, would soon follow in the path he cleared and within years England would be gripped by a frenzy of activity the consequences of which would define the nation's fortunes for succeeding centuries. From a land of simmering potential the country would find a new purpose, as well as the means to realise it, and in doing so become the world's first global economic and military superpower, with the greatest empire the world had ever seen to prove it.

Before all this there was the little matter of a bridge. No ordinary bridge but a magnificent stone construction with three semi-circular spans, the middle one of which stretched fully sixty-three feet. Together the bridge spanned a total of 200 yards, an unbelievable distance, and was fully twelve yards wide. Like its designer, it was bold and simple in appearance, with no external fripperies – there to do a job. The early canal chronicler John Philips later remarked upon the considerable strength of the bridge with *'every front stone [having] five square faces or beds, well jointed and cramped with iron run in with lead … the piers are the largest blocks of stone and camped as before'*. Also like its designer it had hidden depths and solid foundations.

Perhaps most impressively the bridge was suspended thirty-nine feet over the murky black waters of the River Irwell at a place called Barton, an hour's horse ride out from the centre of Manchester. Today, we would pass over such a bridge in our cars without a second glance, but in its day it was a remarkable feat of engineering, made all the more so by the fact that it was not only a bridge but an aqueduct, carrying a self-contained man–made river. Its calm even presence seemed to present a challenge to the more chaotic example nature and God had provided below.

It was this feature that made the construction so special. Much of its importance lay in the questions it posed, not only rational questions but also to the accepted order and God's law. On a purely secular level, no one in England had thought of attempting anything remotely like this structure since Roman times, since when knowledge of how to do such things had been lost. Brindley had, in effect, reinvented the necessary technology. What was more, to those in the know the bridge was only half the achievement. Its construction had required the building of significant embankments on both sides of the river, a task that had required the mobilisation of armies of men equipped with little more than pickaxes and barrows.

One of these embankments, at a place called Stretford Meadows, was over half a mile long and 112 feet in breadth at the base, twenty-four feet at the top, and seventeen feet high. Although this was an age when slavery still thrived overseas, the men who had shifted the tons of earth involved had worked willingly under the direction of the Duke's agent, John Gilbert, and the mere millwright James Brindley.

The structure broke all the rules and defied logic. To the uninitiated and educated alike there was the fundamental question of leakage, for didn't common sense dictate that water always found a way out? Even if it didn't leak, how safe was it? Everyone knew that it had been built in less than a year – by a man whose previous experience was mainly in working with wood, fixing mills. Anyone foolhardy enough to cross the bridge in a boat would at best go aground and at worst suffer a terrifying plunge into the ugly rocks and water below.

This scheme went beyond any Roman aqueduct carrying drinking water, though. It was part of a major new water highway, a canal, capable of carrying cargo in boats as well as men and horses. The bridge had been designed to carry part of a second 'artificial river', free of tides or flow and with smooth straight edges, with a certain imperiousness over the natural conduit that God Himself had supplied to serve that rapidly growing town.

With this bridge man was corralling nature and attempting to tame water, one of her most perfidious agents. The natural order dictated that man should accept what he had been provided with and live with it. Brindley and his bridge challenged that assumption and turned it on its head. What if the will of man could be made to triumph over the will of God? This was radical, even blasphemous thinking, and who knew where it could end? If the natural order could be challenged where would it stop?

Those who felt most threatened that warm summer's day hung onto the belief that the whole thing was the folly of a young and impressionable fool, Francis Egerton, the third Duke of Bridgewater. According to this gossip, this young playboy, whose antics had briefly lit up the London social scene, had been taken in by a convincing charlatan and embarked upon some glorious voyage of self-destruction. The well-known gambler had staked his entire fortune on a venture no one knew the outcome of. He was said to be on the point of bankruptcy.

It was common knowledge that Egerton had been the youngest of the great First Duke's eight children. Gossip in fashionable circles suggested he was the runt of the litter, abandoned by his mother and lacking any formal education for the simple reason that no one had expected

Brindley's path often crossed with that of his contemporary John Smeaton, with the latter's reputation and contrary opinion of Brindley's abilities usually combining to slow Brindley's progress down. (Courtesy of The Waterways Archive)

him to survive. By some freak of chance Egerton had survived all his siblings to inherit both title and lands, an unfortunate state of affairs but these things sometimes happened. Those with an interest in the status quo anticipated a mixture of sorrow and relief as they witnessed his final downfall, along with that of the bridge. Those who had invested their sweat in the project might despair, but the world would go on.

Some later engravings of the aqueduct suggest a backdrop of mills and smoking chimneys, but this is Victorian fancy as James Watt had yet to perfect his steam engine and the Spinning Jenny that would help crown Manchester as 'King Cotton' had yet to be invented. Although large by Georgian standards, Manchester still had a population of less than 20,000 and like many such towns was still largely a place of untapped potential. Isolated from markets beyond its immediate hinterland, the physical realities of geography represented a serious barrier to further growth. Supplying food and fuel to its people remained a major logistical problem, as was maintaining order and keeping the population gainfully occupied.

A mural by the pre-Raphaelite painter Ford Madox-Brown, commissioned in 1878 for Manchester Town Hall, is similarly poetic in its interpretation. In this the foreground is dominated by a broad-beamed boat called the Young Duke, barely under the control of a similarly wide-bottomed young mother wearing her finest dress, a black striped number with puffed sleeves. In the front of the boat sit her infant twins waving blue flags. The air of celebration is echoed on the left hand of the bridge – for the scene depicted is from the top of the aqueduct – where a small brightly liveried band, balanced precariously on the battlements of the bridge and complete with snow-white stockings, is in the process of striking up.

Next to them is another boat upon which stands the Duke of Bridgewater himself, his face innocent and his glass empty, although a fawn-coated Brindley is seen refilling it from the wicker-coated flask of brandy, his so-called 'packet pistol', he was said always to carry with him. The various coats of arms on the Duke's boat are reflected perfectly on the still water. Just in front of them a small boy is preventing a small spaniel from becoming the canal's first victim by fishing it out of the water, sending out the faintest of ripples.

Luckily photographs of the original structure survive, taken just before the aqueduct was demolished not long after Madox-Brown painted his mural. This confirms the main features of the structure as being built of sandstone with two stanchions sitting in the water, each faced with a vertical point, supporting the two main arches. The third, on the southern end, rests on the bank. A wooden wharf sits on the other bank on the Irwell.

These pictures show the aqueduct to be a solid construction, but unremarkable to modern eyes. The distance from the bridge to the Irwell also seems modest – a man could fall down one of the banks and expect to survive. The landscape around the bridge however would have been empty, save for a few trees, which would probably have made the structure stand out in its surroundings. As such, the bridge would have acted as a magnet for the idle and the simply curious on that fine midsummer's morning, who would have walked or ridden to be there.

Amongst them would have been a cross-section of Lancashire society, including local gentlemen farmers and Manchester mill owners, many of whom may have had a few shares in the Mersey & Irwell Navigation Company, which held a monopoly over traffic on the river and would therefore be willing this potential competitor to fail. Members of the clergy would probably have been similarly inclined, although the concerns of some of the more free-thinking amongst their number, who may have been members of some of the informal discussion groups that had recently sprung up, may have been more intellectual than religious.

Others with a more direct stake would have included the men whose dedication and muscles had made the waterway a reality. Many had fled the land to join Brindley's men and would have been unsure if a place remained for them there should the venture fail. Standing alongside them would have been riverboat men, who often had to physically haul their craft up and down the Irwell, dealing with its tides, floods and silt on a daily basis. Despite the direct threat to their livelihood, later, when in the tavern, many of these men would admit to a grudging respect for the men behind the bridge. These river men had witnessed some of the engineering involved, along with its speed and efficiency. Many had benefited from the bribes handed out to forestall them when a particularly delicate piece of work had required Brindley's exclusive access to the river.

If they respected the effort, these men still had grave doubts over the end to which it was directed. To a man, none of them had ever expected the bridge to be completed, fully expecting a flood or the tide to have taken it away each time they passed it. Somehow it had stayed up, but everyone agreed that they were asking for trouble when they filled it with water. It stood practically no chance of surviving.

As it happened they were nearly right. With so much at stake it was hardly surprising that the three main protagonists, Brindley, the Duke and his agent, had agreed that a test run would be a good idea. It turned out just as well they did for when they first ran water into the aqueduct small cracks began to appear in one of the arches. It was at this point that Brindley retired to the Bishop Blaize Tavern at Stretford, presumably in despair, perhaps laying the grounds for the later rumour.

It was left to Gilbert to diagnose the problem – too much weight on the sides of the arch; and also to fix it. Working feverishly, he removed some clay at the weak point and covered the stonework with straw to prevent slippage before applying a fresh layer of clay. Disaster, it seemed, had just been averted.

Despite this, on the day itself it is likely that the Duke, his guest the Earl of Stafford and John Gilbert himself would have shared the anticipation of the crowd as the underwater gates that held the water back were lowered and liquid rushed in to fill the aqueduct. Against a background of hushed anticipation the sound of gushing water would have been clearly audible, its note changing as the channel in the bridge filled slowly. That note would have been a dull one, for the water was pouring into a mud channel, the stonework of the bridge having been covered by a mixture of earth held together by grass and kept firm by clay, giving the bridge the appearance of a furrow held suspended in mid air. Looking from the side it would have been easy to forget it was a bridge at all.

With a slight twist of his head the Duke would have been able to spot the silhouette of a horse emerging out of the late morning mist about a hundred yards down the water, growing larger as it approached the bridge. Attached to a harness on its back was a rope trailing out lazily to a flat bottomed barge carrying a load of coal, exactly the same sort of barge people were more used to seeing plying the river below. The Duke's men had held a ballot to decide who would have the honour of leading the horse and the winner held no fear as he advanced slowly.

As he approached, the Duke would probably have been reminded of the words of the engineer John Smeaton who, in a rare moment of doubt he had allowed to examine the plans for the aqueduct and pass his opinion. It had not been favourable. To his face, this expert, no stranger to lofty structures, for he had recently completed the Eddystone Lighthouse, had pronounced that *'I have often heard of castles in the air; but never before saw where any of them were to be erected'*. After a moment of doubt, the Duke had followed his instincts, convinced by Brindley's absolute certainty that he was right. That trust remained a gamble.

Suddenly the rest of the crowd noticed the approaching barge, their attention drawn more by the clanking of the horse's harness than the soundless progress of the boat, discernable only by the slight V-shaped ripple thrown out by its bow. It is easy to imagine a gasp going up as the man leading it reassured the horse with a pat to its flanks as they stepped onto the battlements of the bridge and apparently walked across a stone tightrope.

Applause might have started somewhere to the left of the Duke and grown spontaneously until it developed into a crescendo, augmented by whoops and cheers. Hats would have been thrown into the air and all sense of social hierarchy would, at that point, have collapsed as men great and small, carried along by the moment, queued to shake the Duke's hand. Wherever he was, Brindley might have allowed himself a slight smile.

Soon others followed the horseman onto the bridge, testing their luck and bravery. Other boats floated out over the river, some making the journey back and forth several times, with the more enterprising boatmen even starting to charge for taking passengers. Over the middle span it was possible to see a man being dangled by his ankles over the side of the bridge, occasioning further gasps from the women in the crowd, whilst a colleague stood to one side holding his waistcoat and hat.

This was the correspondent of the Manchester Mercury, and he was later to file the following despatch: *'A large boat carrying upwards of fifty tons was towed along the new part of the*

Canal over arches across the River Irwell which were so firm, secure and compact that not a single drop of water could be perceived to ooze out of any part of them.' His colleague, commenting on the wider implications of what he'd seen suggested slightly less enthusiastically that, *'The Canal will be of very great use as well as amusement'*.

The three men behind the Duke's Cut, soon to be renamed the Bridgewater Canal, had issued a statement of intent: canals represented the future. But that intent needed to be implemented. Finishing this first canal and making money from it was to preoccupy both the Duke and his agent for a few years yet. It fell to Brindley, the master of water, to realise the potential they had unleashed that day, to digest the lessons learned and to form and implement a much grander vision: one of a network of canals that would link the nation and bind together a disparate population in a way that allowed them to realise their latent collective energies.

Who then was this man and what made him so special? What were the qualities that drove him on and allowed him to succeed where others had previously failed? What right has he to be called the man who united the kingdom?

The journey to answering these questions takes in success and failure, aristocrats and navvies, dramatic changes in circumstance, both personal and financial and, as we have already seen, some of the most daring challenges to conventional wisdom ever suggested. It is a journey that begins unpromisingly in a damp stone church in the Staffordshire Moorlands.

one

Family Ties

It is Easter Day, the most significant point in the Church calendar, in the year 1664, the year before the Black Death was set to lay Europe low. The local people are gathering at the local parish church, St Edward's. It is the only church in the Staffordshire town of Leek and it proclaims its position proudly from the top of the hill that is Mill Lane. Solidly built out of local red sandstone it had, until the dissolution of the monasteries, been attached to the local Abbey of Dieulacres whose presence had dominated the local community.

The congregation inside on this unseasonably warm day is obediently silent as the local priest George Rhodes makes the sign of the cross over the sacrament. There is only a slight rustling amongst those standing and crouching on the cold stone floor as they shuffle to get more comfortable.

Motes of dust dance lazily in the rays of sunshine that angle in from the rose window. Although the day outside is a good one, inside the darkness is leavened only by the burst of colour seeping through the stained glass above, an unusually ornate feature for such a plain town. A respectful silence descends. Heightened senses can just detect the scent of the best of what remained of last year's hay, scattered that morning on the floor.

The Reverend Rhodes turns to his flock, raises the host and makes to speak. The next voice everyone hears is not his, however, but that of a young woman, dressed all in black, who has risen from the floor in the centre of the church. A hat hides her hair and her plain long skirt scrapes the floor. The Reverend Rhodes casts his face up to the beautifully crafted ceiling of the nave in frustration. His eyes briefly take in the magnificence of its ornately carved wooden roses sitting at the intersection of solid oak beams, which in turn rest on plain white corbels.

The woman's name is Alice Bowman and she is a known troublemaker. Some know her better as a dissenter. Before that moment few had noticed her, she rarely if ever went to church. The fact that she was there at all should have been enough to signal trouble. Sighs fill the air as she stands and points her finger round the congregation.

'Reject these mere symbols of faith!', she proclaims, her voice strong and absent of doubt. 'Reveal thy inner Christ!'

Brindley. (Courtesy of The Waterways Archive)

A few frustrated murmurings echo around the main body of the church. The service is long enough without interruptions, there's much to be done at home, day of rest or not. The Reverend, shaken out of his reverie, begins to recover, but not fast enough. A few of the congregation start to rise. The Reverend pauses.

'Reject this finery and ceremony', Alice continues, gaining yet more confidence despite the gathering menace. 'Ye have no need of priests and robes!' This last pronouncement is, it seems, the final straw for the party advancing towards her, although in truth Alice's fate had probably been sealed the moment she'd stood up. A deep cry goes up, one tinged with anger and venom.

'Grab her!'

Despite the priest's half-hearted protestations half a dozen of the larger members of his flock descend upon Alice and lift her from the ground, two on each thrashing leg and one on each arm. A cheer goes up, destroying the atmosphere of peace and due reverence that had pervaded the church less than a minute before.

There is a loud wooden thump as the door is pulled open and crashes on its jamb. Alice continues to declaim her beliefs, but her voice has become more distant, stop she is pushed face downwards into the soft, drying mud outside. It is only when her infant son, left behind in the melee and stranded on a small knitted rug on the floor, starts to cry that people realise that she had not come alone.

★ ★ ★ ★ ★ ★ ★ ★ ★

These days the moorlands of north Staffordshire are a magnet for tourism, but even today it is easy to imagine how, at the end of the seventeenth century, they would have been a bleak and uninviting place, especially if you had to eke a living out of them. Men and women worked hard to ensure survival for themselves and their families and could go for days without seeing someone outside their immediate kin, let alone figures of authority such as the local lord or clergyman. Villages were barely more than loose collections of houses, and towns were an abstract notion for most.

A contemporary record describes the climate of that part of the county as *'cold and wet, like that of the adjacent parts of Derbyshire and Cheshire; snow lies long on the moorlands and the west wind seldom fails to bring rain'*. The most noticeable feature to someone new to the area would indeed have been the wind that raged off the moors, a constant whistle oscillating in pitch, that seemed to send a rasping, cleansing draught through the landscape.

It is perhaps unsurprising therefore that Brindley's maternal great-grandparents, Alice and Henry Bowman, were early members of the Society of Friends, or Quakers, with its emphasis on the simple life, on unadorned worship and the rejection of creeds and priests. Those who adopted the Society's ways chose also to stand out from the crowd, but the self-righteousness and spiritual certainty of the early Quakers no doubt gave some kind of comfort against their self-inflicted ostracism from their neighbours. They would have needed it. With memories of the Civil War still raw this was not a good time to be different.

What was more, their absence from church and subsequent refusal to pay tithes seemed to accentuate their determination to be seen as somehow special. Although they may have regarded all men as equal, going so far as to refuse to take their hats off in court, this was still an age when some were more equal than others and prudent so-called dissenters would have needed constant looks over their shoulder when they walked home down tracks lit only by the moon. Fatal clashes were not unknown and probably went unpunished.

The Bowmans were not exempt from punishment for challenging the prevailing orthodoxy. Three years before Alice's outburst at St Edward's her husband Henry had spent a year and seven months in jail for refusing to pay tithes. Quakers believed that no man had a prior call on another. Alice's ejection cost her a spell in the local House of Correction and it cost her infant son Matthew, still suckling his mother, his life – prison being no place for an infant. No price, it would seem, was too high for her principles.

This behaviour would have seemed very strange to Alice's father and indeed her grandfather, both of whom could legitimately describe themselves in their lifetimes as Gentlemen. Neither lord nor yeoman, this title described a man of independent means, a sort of incipient middle class. Alice's grandfather Samuel Stubbs had had property to his name and been a relatively wealthy and well-read lawyer, who had practised in Tunstall in Staffordshire and had even represented clients in London. Her father Walter was said to live modestly, but his will showed he had the distinction of owning more animals than his neighbours.

Both had died before Alice married and perhaps it was this freedom from family influence, and the general air of rebelliousness around at the time, that gave her the confidence to make her own mark. It was 1658, when the country was still being ruled as a King-less Commonwealth and at a time when her cousin was a local rector, that Alice had became a Quaker.

Occasional lapses into defiant anarchy beside, despite their aversion to material goods, those of Alice's children who survived infancy and adolescence maintained the family tradition of a steady and unostentatious accumulation of wealth. In time, Alice's sons purchased and developed farms in the surrounding areas, becoming particularly skilled in animal husbandry, notably with sheep, but also with pigs, cows and goats. When he died in 1714, Alice's eldest son was worth over £1,000, twice the amount she herself had left a quarter of a century before.

Her eldest daughter Ellen, however, was another story. It may have been in the blood, because Ellen too appeared determined to plough her own furrow. Her act of rebellion however was to marry beneath her. By so doing she created her own version of the ancient story of maternal disapproval of a daughter's choice of life partner. Although probably a Quaker too – marriage outside the faith would have been a step too far – Ellen's new husband Joseph Brindley was very clearly *persona non grata* with his mother-in-law. When she died Ellen was left the princely sum of £40 by her mother, and although enough at the time for a working man to just about support a family for a year, this was half the amount left to her unmarried sisters.

On its own this is not that remarkable, after all Ellen had probably already benefited from a marriage settlement. What were unusual, however, were the strings to which the inheritance was very firmly attached. Alice's will stated specifically that the money was to be used solely for the maintenance of Ellen and her children, that it be held by Ellen's brother and that if she went to court to challenge the will she would get nothing. The message could not have been clearer: Joseph was not to be allowed within a mile of the money.

The reasons behind this rift are not known. Little is known of Joseph's background, Brindley actually being a rather common name in Staffordshire at the time. Whatever the reasons, the suspicion must be that Joseph's enthusiasm for Quakerism didn't match that of his wife's family. Ellen was the only one of her siblings not to be buried a Quaker and their oldest son James, father of our James, gained something of a reputation for betting and practising country sports with those who could afford to pursue them, suggesting he was hardly brought up in a strict Quaker household.

Whatever his faults though, James was Ellen's only son and it seems her family was prepared to forgive him his parentage and take him to their bosom, perhaps in the hope of providing the spiritual guidance they suspected he was not getting at home. His predilection for play over work clearly grated with their Quaker ideals. James senior spent some of his boyhood years at the family's modest estate, probably more of a large farm, at Stockley Park in Tutley, Staffordshire and learnt farming from his Uncle Harry, Ellen's older brother.

Despite these good intentions, if the aim was to redeem James it seems they largely failed. At the age of thirty-one he got married to one Susanna Bradbury. This was a rushed affair and a second attempt to complete the ceremony. The first had been scheduled for the famous crooked-spire church of Chesterfield, fully thirty miles away, suggesting a need for secrecy. What is certain is that parental consent was not given and James omitted to bring a friend or relative with him to complete the marriage bond, causing the whole enterprise to be abandoned.

Three months later, in January 1716 they tried again. Once more there was no parental consent, but this time it didn't matter, with Susanna having turned twenty-one in the interim. The reason for this haste became clear when James junior was born a few months later. There is also a suspicion that Susannah wasn't a Quaker, which if true would have cast further despair on his grandmother's family. It was in these unpromising circumstances that the man who transformed his nation, and by extension the world, was born.

* * * * * * * * * *

Fresh fencing has recently been installed around Brindley's birthplace, where the tree grows which replaced the original ash that broke the flags of his parents' cottage.

James Brindley's later success certainly can't be put down to any advantage bestowed at birth. Although his wider family were relatively well to do, they owned their own land and had capital, his parents had cast themselves firmly as the black sheep of the family. They lived more than a full day's walk away from the family farm and not even in the same county – effectively in a different country.

The cottage where James first saw the light of day no longer exists, but its location is marked both by a modest black plaque and a tree, in an unprepossessing hamlet called Tunstead, near Wormhill in north Derbyshire, about three miles outside Buxton. Even three-quarters of a century later Wormhill had only twenty-nine houses and was described as a hamlet with a chapel. Tunstead was appreciably smaller, possibly no more than two or three cottages grouped together for convenience rather than through any true sense of community.

No more than six inches by eight, the plaque in Tunstead has weathered significantly over the years and become quite difficult to read. A small stockade fence has recently been erected to make access easier. When you get closer it is just possible to make out the following words:

James Brindley 1716–1772, Millwright and Civil Engineer.
Here stood the cottage in which James Brindley was born. Of humble birth, he became famous as the pioneer builder of the great canals of England. This plaque was erected by the local history section of the Derbyshire Archaeological Society unveiled by J.L. Longland Esq. MA on November 1st 1958 and Miss Y.H.B. Hartford planted the adjacent ash tree.

Such a message befits the man. It is simple, states the facts and hints at greatness without making any undue claims.

The tree replaced an original ash that had grown up through the flags of the floor of a cottage that long before had fallen derelict. The Brindleys were the last to inhabit this modest dwelling and after they left its stones were ignominiously removed to build cowsheds. At one time a labourer was sent to clear a path to the neighbouring farmhouse but was reluctant to fell a healthy sapling. As a consequence it was left and fittingly acted as Brindley's only memorial for many decades.

Like most at the time, the Brindley's home would have been a modest affair, rented from a local landowner. Its focal point would have been the fire, which was almost a room to itself with seats built into the chimney so all could enjoy what little warmth it threw out. Wood was the primary fuel, coal being a luxury almost unheard of. Peat would have been an option for some, but in the open Derbyshire countryside even that was in short supply, hoarded for use in winter and used only for cooking in summer.

The world James Brindley was born into, or more specifically the country, was still recovering from a period of relative uncertainty. Only fifty years before, the nation had been ravaged by the plague and the population was still only just recovering. Fear of its return still hung over most families' heads, with the young and old the most vulnerable to disease, the great leveller. During Brindley's youth the population of England, around five million at the time, actually fell by 100,000, due in large part to a series of epidemics of influenza and fevers, usually typhoid or smallpox. Rumours of a resurgence of the Black Death, usually centred on France, were commonplace.

And yet there were signs that things were changing. Two years before James' birth the Georgian dynasty had begun with the accession of George I. This was secured a year later with the defeat of the Great Pretender while three years before in 1713 The Treaty of Utrecht had ended the crushingly expensive War of Spanish Succession. London, that great cauldron of activity, was growing at an exponential rate and was already in the process of becoming a consumer-led economic phenomenon.

It would be wrong to say though that England had suddenly become a settled nation, looking forward to a period of unbroken peace and prosperity. For a start the idea of a single nation was an abstract one, with few wandering much beyond a few miles of their birthplace in their entire lifetime. With only a few exceptions, such as Norwich, Bristol or Exeter, London dominated commerce. In population terms alone it dwarfed its nearest rivals by a factor of ten. Few of the market towns that acted as local gathering places had a population of much more than a thousand. The country at this time was like a random ink splat upon a page, the one big dot of London with a series of minor dots representing a series of unconnected communities.

Furthermore, getting around the country was nigh on impossible by any means other than foot or horse, the latter a luxury afforded only to the few. Although there was the semblance of a road system, improving slowly through the introduction of turnpikes, an early form of toll road, the highways were subject to disrepair and vulnerable to crime and adverse weather. They were mud bowls in winter and dust traps in summer.

No one could be sure that the Catholic threat was gone forever and, as we have seen, the presence of non-Conformists such as the Quakers remained disconcerting to many. In addition, the political system was only just beginning to get itself together. It had taken the bursting of the South Sea Bubble in 1720 to shock politicians into action. Given the role of many of them in inflating the bubble, it was in the interests of few for the true history of that scandal to be revealed. Accordingly, in-fighting was abandoned in favour of co-operation and self-preservation.

The war, although expensive, had fuelled an economic boom through the demand for naval and military supplies. Suddenly that demand ceased, and with it the good times. As is often the way, the 'peace dividend' proved elusive. One good side-effect of the South Sea Bubble was that it helped to force some realism into the economy.

And yet, despite all this, there were signs of optimism. Although low corn prices through the 1720s and 30s meant that making money from the land wasn't easy, productivity increased during this period to the point where the country quite comfortably fed itself and even became a net food exporter. There was also a sense of social mobility within England that was absent over the channel. It was worthwhile for the ambitious to strive, rags to riches stories were not fairy tales and examples existed of considerable fortunes being made. Whilst the aristocracy still by and large governed, they displayed remarkable pragmatism in welcoming new entrants to their ranks. Unlike some European systems there was less sense of caste, of being born into a position and being unable to change it.

Also unlike its continental counterparts England more or less enjoyed a single tongue, a single rule of law and a single King. Spiritually then, if not tangibly, this was a United Kingdom even if, despite the Act of Union in 1707, an eye still needed to kept on the Scots, as came to be amply demonstrated by the exploits of the Young Pretender and his eventual defeat at Culloden in 1746. Although still small, the towns and cities across the land were beginning to exert their own identity, encouraged in part by the success of London, which they sought both to mimic and, in their own small way, rival.

A native inventiveness was demonstrating itself more confidently. Local and regional crafts and industries were encouraged to prosper, in part by the demand emanating from the towns and in part by a growing understanding of how manufacturing could be made more efficient, although this remained home based rather than organised in factories.

Pockets of collectivised industry did exist, not least in iron working and coal mining, their location determined by the availability of natural resources. Given the abundance of such resources the country was blessed with however, this potential had hardly been scratched. The energies lying recumbent outside London were looking for something to harness them.

In reality the economy was winding up like a spring, waiting for something to unleash it. Political, social and economic conditions in the country were coming into line but they needed some kind of catalyst to bring them together and make sense of them.

* * * * * * * * * *

All these forces would have meant little to small tenant farmers like James Brindley senior. Although there were newspapers around at the time they were mainly an urban phenomenon, and anyway few could read. Most news was spread by word of mouth, but this meant little you rarely even saw your neighbour.

For the vast majority of the population life remained a precarious business. Like most people the Brindleys would have started each day by opening the door and glancing towards the heavens, not so much out of any sense of piety but, in solid English tradition, to check the skies. The weather and the seasons still held the power over life and death for some and the difference between living and merely surviving for most. Although cases of actual starvation were unusual, young James' early years would have been a worrying time for his parents, who would have wished rather than expected him to make each subsequent birthday.

The scene that would have greeted them every morning would have been overwhelmingly green, with splashes of the local grey from the dry stone walls that marked out the field systems and gave the whole landscape a marbled effect. In the near distance a ridge ran down from left to right, its top defined by a line of trees.

Their small cottage was perched on a slight incline, a rough track outside leading to a more substantial road, still not much more than a sheep track, that would, if followed one way, take them into Buxton and if followed the other into a place called Tideswell. Of the two the latter would have been bigger, but probably still little more than a large hamlet. Then, as now, the scenery would have been punctuated by clumps of angular rock buried into the grass, breaking free like new teeth, providing useful places to shelter, to sit and have lunch, or perhaps, if you were younger, to hide behind.

Like most young couples the Brindleys would have worked together in the fields out of economic necessity. In the absence of local relatives to look after him young James probably went with them or watched from the sidelines. As a family, their year would have been dictated by a rhythm of ploughing, sowing and harvesting, their days by baking bread, milking, churning and preserving.

Undernourished and perpetually tired, the Brindleys made their way, open to the vicissitudes and price fluctuations of the agrarian economy, but surviving. Falls and rises in the population impacted upon the demand for food and this, coupled with the unpredictability of Mother Nature, meant that few families could plan ahead with any certainty. It is possible that James, like many other children at this time, was physically sewn into his clothes for the winter. Men changed their shirts only once a week.

Whatever the depravations of their lot, English tenant farmers like the Brindleys were at least better off than their European counterparts, many of whom lived either as serfs, little better than slaves, or firmly under the yoke of a feudal lord. An Englishman could at least starve a free man. Living off the land had been made possible by a creeping programme of enclosures in the preceding decades that had opened the door for the tenant farmer.

Just because it was possible, however, didn't necessarily make it viable. Small-scale farmers like the Brindleys were at the vanguard of changes taking place in farming, and it was very much a time of sink or swim. Things were changing, but too slowly to be noticed on a day-to-day, year-on-year level. During Brindley's lifetime there were almost as many advances in tools and techniques in agriculture as there were in industry, but as a family they would have benefited only marginally.

In the outside world this was a society where slavery was seen as perfectly natural, and an Englishman still had the right to beat his wife – provided the stick he used was no thicker than his thumb (the origin of the phrase 'rule of thumb'). There were also occasional incidences of wife sales, with spouses sometimes traded for an ox, as an early form of divorce.

This extract from one of Brindley's journals shows how he meticulously kept a record of his time and expenses in later life. (Courtesy of The Institution of Civil Engineers)

James Brindley senior had already proved his willingness to resist convention. Faced with a choice between hard work and hedonism, the latter usually won. It was relatively easy for him to lose himself in the open uncultivated grasslands around his homestead; no one was around to spy on him. His passion seemed to be country sports. Samuel Smiles, a Victorian biographer, also suggests that *'if there was a bull running within twenty miles he was sure to be there'*. Smiles also noted that the district bullring lay less than three miles away and the road to it passed almost by his door. The temptation must at times have been irresistible.

It is doubtful whether Susannah would have regarded the odd brace of birds or a rabbit sufficient compensation for her husband's absences, but what choice did she have? Before he was five James had been joined by two brothers, Joseph and John, and by then Susannah's life would, by modern standards at least, have been intolerable.

Close to poverty she effectively had to keep the household together. Women in her situation regularly took on extra jobs, some of which would have been quite skilled such as glove making or straw plaiting to even out seasonal variations in earnings, to pay the rent and generally to make ends meet. Poaching or even petty theft were also widespread if inadvisable, for there were over 200 capital offences in the early eighteenth century, most of them connected with stealing, the removal of property being at least as significant a crime against society and the natural order as the removal of life.

With no sign of a reconciliation with the main branch of the family, James and Susannah continued to live in their modest dwelling in Tunstead with their family. Resigned to their lot, Susannah began to turn her thoughts to educating her eldest son. This would have taken the form of basic learning for life rather than anything formal. It is unlikely that Susannah would have known how to write, as she did not even sign her own marriage certificate. Nursery rhymes would have taught morality from an early age and passed on the rudiments of counting. Decks of cards would have helped with basic numeracy and letters would have been learned through familiarisation of inscriptions rather than books.

An inability to read and write would have been perfectly normal for a child of James' background, and although sometimes described as illiterate it is probably fairer to say that he had only a rudimentary grasp of the language. His later journals demonstrate a phonetic grasp of words, but this needs to be put into the context of a language that was yet to have its first published dictionary.

We can only speculate on what James junior would have made of his surroundings. It is said that he was a solitary boy, preferring his own company and showing a particular aptitude for whittling sticks. It's tempting though to conjure up an image of a withdrawn child sitting against the wall of the house watching his loveable rogue father come and go and his mother struggle to keep the household functioning. The demands of his younger brothers would have deflected attention from him and provided the space to observe and think, even if he had to work while he did so.

During this time young Brindley would have learned valuable practical skills, notably in husbandry and in the more general skills of self-sufficiency and survival, a need exacerbated by his father's frequent absences. It is equally likely that he also gained a love of working in the open air, although a life spent largely outside would have been normal for a child of his age at the time. It is equally possible however, given the example set before him and his contemplative ways, that the first seeds of doubt were being sown over whether farming was really what he wanted to spend the rest of his life doing.

* * * * * * * * * *

When James was around ten a sudden change took place in his family's circumstances. The daily grind of life at Tunstead was replaced by a return from exile and residence at one of the family's farms at Lowe Hill, near Leek. This event had been precipitated by Richard Bowman, James Brindley senior's now ageing uncle, brother of the Uncle Harry who had taken him under his wing in his youth.

Lowe Hill would appear to have been a definite step up in the world for the Brindleys, being a more substantial property held freehold by Richard Bowman and described later in his will as 'his estate'. The countryside was also more appealing, being greener and more organised, with clear field patterns and more trees. There was a slight sting in the tail of the homecoming however, in that James Brindley senior had to provide a pension for his mother, the notorious Ellen, but at £2 a year this would have been a small price to pay.

We can only speculate on the reasons behind this reversal in fortunes, but it seems reasonable to conclude that Richard Bowman was eager to put his affairs, and those of his immediate family, in order before he died. Perhaps intimations of mortality, combined with the conscience of his faith, led him to want to patch up the most glaring gap in his family's fabric. If these were his motives he proved to be a prescient man for Richard was to die six years before his sister and it would seem that moving to Lowe Hill turned out to be the making of James Brindley senior.

By this time the prodigal James had probably turned forty, an even more significant milestone in the early eighteenth century than it is now, and the time had come for him finally to grow up. Whilst it may be acceptable to be a jack the lad through your thirties there comes a time when it starts to become a bit pathetic. Perhaps he had simply hit that time most men reach in their lives when they stare at themselves in the mirror and ask where they're going even if before the move it is highly unlikely that he'd have owned a mirror.

Whatever the reasons for the move, Susannah must have breathed a huge sigh of relief, for here was the chance finally to make something of their lives. At the same time it must have been difficult for her to throw her lot in with, and be beholden to, her husband's family, a family that had largely ostracised them for ten years. From a life of relative isolation she was pitched into a situation where she had to exercise social skills and diplomacy, a non-Quaker amongst Quakers, with all their strange attendant ways.

By now Susannah probably had at least half a dozen children to contend with, the first three boys being followed by two daughters, Esther and Ann, before another boy, Henry, who was probably born after the move. What is certain is that Susannah's youngest child, another girl, was baptised Mary at St Edward's in 1731.

The good news, however, was that her husband seemed to have knuckled down to his responsibilities. Presented with a test case on how to farm successfully, James senior seems to have picked up the cudgels and started, albeit rather late in life, the process of making a success of himself. It helped of course that he had more or less been handed Lowe Hill on a plate, but perhaps that was what had been needed. *De facto* ownership became *de jure* when two-thirds of the property was left to him in Richard Bowman's will in 1728, the other third being left to his sister Hannah, which in time he bought off her.

James Brindley senior was to live a further thirty-five years and to die at Lowe Hill, a comfortably well-off and respected member of the community. In his will he left a number of bequests, including the sum of £150 a year to his son and his male heirs as well as £30 a year for each of his other children. In the event James junior had little chance to enjoy his inheritance, dying himself within a couple of years of his father, but this is to race ahead in our story.

Relieved of the immediate threat of poverty, the Brindley family began to enjoy their new status, even if it did mean sharing a house for a further six years with the notorious Ellen Bowman. James junior's life would have improved immeasurably, with one significant change being a chance to indulge in some formal education at the local Quaker's Meeting House. It is not known for certain that James attended the school, but there is a record of a resolution to admit non-Quakers, as James would have been, to the school, and it seems unlikely that given the influence of Ellen Bowman he would have been refused.

At the same time, James was encouraged to earn a living both in fulfilment of Quaker beliefs in thrift and hard work and to make a contribution to the household income. The Brindleys were not so well off now that they could afford to carry their teenage children. Thus James Brindley found himself engaged on various labouring jobs, probably helping to crystallise for him what it was he wanted to do with his life.

These jobs reinforced his desire to turn his hands to practical matters. By now he had graduated from whittling sticks to modelling small mechanical devices out of wood. Some early accounts of Brindley's life suggest that he liked nothing better than to visit local mills and examine how they worked, coming back to make models of the machinery such as water-wheels and cogs for his own amusement. These stories seem overly convenient, but something must have happened to plant seeds of doubt over what would have otherwise been his natural, and for most, rather inviting destiny, that of inheriting the farm.

The event that probably changed Brindley's life forever was the death of his grandmother Ellen. Upon her passing the maintenance payments secured by the careful planning of her brother Richard would have ceased. At the same time her own property at Yoxall towards Litchfield, thirty miles away, described as a house with a barn and three closes of land, would have been divided between James senior and his two surviving sisters.

For the Brindley family Ellen's death represented the end of one era and the beginning of another. Their eldest son was now seventeen and ready to make his own way in the world. For James this meant going to Macclesfield, just over the border in Cheshire, to take up an apprenticeship as a millwright. It would seem that he had made his case convincingly enough to persuade his parents that he should pursue his apparent talent for all things mechanical rather than take on the farm. It's likely that this had been obvious for some time, but the death of his grandmother Ellen had freed up the cash to make it possible. It was now up to him to prove that he was right.

two

From Bungler to Master

At around ten miles, for a fit young man the walk just over the border to his new home would not have been that onerous. It was still winter, however, and the roads were probably slippery underfoot with mud, causing Brindley to walk a bit slower than he might have done otherwise. Carrying a small bundle with his clothes and a few belongings, he would have made light work of the trek uphill out of Staffordshire, across the River Dane that marked the county border and then down again into Sutton, a village two miles outside Macclesfield.

The landscape he crossed would have been quite alien to him, deepening the impression of passing into new territory. The moorlands would have been vast and bleak, stretching for miles with only an occasional vertical shaft of smoke indicating a distant crofter's cottage. He probably met no one on his trek, pausing occasionally to refresh himself in one of the many small brooks that gabbled down the hills, perhaps tossing a few blades of grass into the water to see them race.

The scenery would have been daunting, apparently stretching the moors into infinity. Steep precipices would have meant he would have had to watch his step carefully. The only signs of life would have been a few scraggy sheep, barely loved by their owners as their fleeces were too coarse for clothing and too short for combing. Sharp angular peaks would have guarded the horizon, washed over by dark wispy clouds that skipped across the sky and occasionally hid their tops. From time to time these clouds would gather together and burst, sending a sudden isolated shower of rain, to be watched or avoided if possible, although shelter was practically impossible given the lack of trees.

After these showers bright sunshine would often follow, appearing as suddenly as the rain and undoing their nuisance. The ground beneath would have been springy and wet, but despite this, and the time of year, the landscape would have looked scorched and brown because of the spiky reeds that grew up from the bogs below. Dips and ditches, valleys and hillocks, this was nature in the raw painted on a wide canvas. Here and there the brown-green of the grass would be alleviated by a splash of grey scree, clinging to a hillside like spilt plaster.

ON THESE PREMISES
1733~1740
JAMES BRINDLEY,
THE FAMOUS CIVIL ENGINEER
AND CANAL BUILDER, SERVED
AS APPRENTICE TO ABRAHAM
BENNETT.

Brindley's early apprenticeship is marked by this simple sign above Bennett's workshop in Sutton Lane Ends.

On arriving at the workshop young James would have been relieved to see a vigorous brook running parallel to the house across the way from the track outside. Between eight to ten feet wide, its incessant babbling would have been a welcome and reassuring sound for him to fall asleep to at night. The workshop and the brook are still there. The workshop is now a single garage, albeit a deep one, to a good-sized house whose local brown stones have been painted white. A simple stone plaque above the workshop states the bare facts:

> *On these premises 1733–1740 James Brindley, the famous civil engineer and canal builder served as apprentice to Abraham Bennett.*

As he made his way towards the door for the first time all sorts of thoughts were probably running through young James' head, almost certainly a mixture of excitement and trepidation. On the one hand this was what he had argued for and wanted. Like many a young man before and since he had been looking for his ticket out of the family home and the opportunity to stretch himself in a new environment. Although most seventeen year olds probably think their family a bit odd, James Brindley had more cause to than most.

On the other hand he was entering unknown territory. He would be living with people he had never met before and initially at least he was on trial only. What if he didn't measure up? The prospect of trudging those ten miles back home with his tail between his legs would have been an unappetising one. These would only have been misgivings however, not doubts. Entering into an apprenticeship was still very much the done thing for promising young men like James Brindley. Success at a chosen trade tended to map out a secure career path that would define their future life.

Upon completing seven years apprenticeship they could hope to become a journeyman, a status that would position them well in the marriage market. A few years more and they might hope to become a master themselves. With their own business, whether they thrived or merely survived would depend upon how good they were at their trade, how hard they worked and how well they performed as businessmen. Unless they were particularly incompetent or unlucky, or as many did, if they succumbed to drink, they could reasonably expect security from poverty and a level of relative prosperity.

The trial period was therefore especially critical for James. Even if he survived that, the seven-year term was not going to be a cakewalk. Apprentices were usually seen as a form of cheap, near slave labour, who wouldn't dare to gainsay their master, even if they were wrong. A rejected apprentice would be labelled a troublemaker and find it nigh on impossible to find fresh indentures. Some masters were known to beat their apprentices, who had no choice but to take their punishment. As another mouth to feed, most would not have been welcomed back by their families even if they did manage to escape.

Food and lodging would have been another concern for Brindley as he started the gentle climb down into Sutton. Both represented a cost to the master and could be trimmed according to circumstances. The people he was expected to work with would also have been a worry as his new master also employed a number of journeymen. James had had very little exposure to young non-Quaker men of his own age, and was used to being the eldest. His coping skills were to be tested to the limit. Suddenly he was to be the new boy, the goat, and fair game for anyone with a bent for cruelty or practical jokes. On top of all that his father would have taken endless pleasure in the preceding few days in scaring him with tales of possible initiation ceremonies.

The most critical unknown would have been the nature of his new master, one Abraham Bennett, wheelwright and millwright. On arrival, Brindley must have quickly felt a sense of *déjà vu*. Like his father when he was growing up his master was rarely to be seen. Having reached a certain level of success, Bennett was usually to be found in the local inn. Even when he was in the workshop he abrogated his responsibilities to pass on the secrets of his trade, preferring instead to employ Brindley as a runner to the inn to fetch fresh supplies of beer.

As a result, Brindley was left to learn through experiment and, where possible, observation. With the journeymen often out on jobs and the master away at the inn he would find himself left in sole charge of the workshop. With his enquiring mind the array of tools and materials at his disposal would have provided a classroom for self-education.

Although Brindley probably welcomed the solitude of the empty workshop, his situation was far from ideal. The seven years before him must have seemed like a sentence, and one he was going to emerge from only half-taught if things carried on in this way. The alternative however, the noise and bustle of a busy yard and the taunting of his workmates, would have been a high price to pay for learning. Those around him would have treated him with little more than contempt, for as an apprentice he represented a possible future competitor in a limited market. He needed to earn their respect, but was given no opportunities to do so.

The language in the workshop would have been either incomprehensible, with different and previously unheard accents or, where it was understandable, it would usually have been coarse and probably quite shocking for a boy brought up in a Quaker-influenced family. New words and oaths would have cut through the air like a scythe, causing him to flush and try to hide his barely shaven face in case anyone saw and took the opportunity to heap further ridicule.

It is perhaps unsurprising that Brindley took a while to find his feet, let alone to shine. Bennett at first thought him slow and probably a bit backward. Learning through trial and error meant he had to make mistakes, and quite naturally, given the environment he was in, it was these that were noticed rather than any successes. Left alone in the workshop he had to do the best he could when casual callers came in for a quick repair. The result was often complaints from the customers and a mouthful of abuse from the journeymen when they returned to find their tools blunted and precious wood spoiled.

His first two years at Bennett's workshop would have been little short of a disaster for Brindley, constantly on the brink of being sent home to a life of general labouring, his dreams in shatters. The final ignominy came when he acquired the nickname of 'the bungler'. One incident in particular sums up this period. On a rare occasion when he was actually given a job to do, Brindley quite naturally sought to impress. The task was a simple one, to fit the spokes to a cartwheel – a standard wheelwright task.

Diligently he worked away, fitting each spoke separately and fashioning them to fit the holes he had cleared on the wheel. It was only when he applied the gauge stick, a piece of wood attached temporarily to the wheel hub to ensure consistent measurement, that he realised that he had fitted all the spokes leaning in instead of out, giving it a bowlegged appearance and ruining the wheel. To have failed so comprehensively in such a basic job must have made Bennett despair. The language and derision Brindley must have endured after this incident would have been almost impossible to endure, and it is easy to imagine him crying himself to sleep most nights, despite his years.

If there was some doubt about his ability to complete his apprenticeship as a millwright, during these years Brindley was at least learning from the school of hard knocks. Despite the cold shoulder he received from his fellow workers and the lack of formal training from his master some knowledge was permeating his brain.

Wrights of whatever description were the general jacks of all trades of their local areas. Their main skills were their facility in working with different materials, although wood still dominated, and the ability to think on their feet. In an age when labour was plentiful there was little incentive to invent new labour-saving machinery, and as a result the tools of the wrights' trade were the basic ones of saw, chisel, foot lathe and anvil, as they had been for centuries.

These were practical men, marinated in experience and seasoned with dexterity. Separated from other tradesmen by geography, they were self-reliant men, learning as they went the skills of mechanics, carpenters and early engineers. They were also valuable members of the communities they operated in, making life more tolerable through their ability to fix problems large and small, an important contribution if their skills meant bringing a valued piece of agricultural or industrial machinery back into service. Millwrights in particular enjoyed a high status within these communities and had to acquire additional skills such as an ease with machinery and a natural appreciation of the topography of landscapes – essential when calculating where best to locate a water or windmill for example.

Given his natural predilection towards the practical it seems that some of these qualities did start to rub off on Brindley. The turning point seemed to come in the autumn of 1735, two-and-a-half years into the apprenticeship. Notice came to the workshop of a fire at a silk mill in Macclesfield that had caused particular damage to the main shaft bearing. With everyone else busy Bennett had no choice but to send Brindley.

This was his big chance and he was determined not to blow it. Sent to inspect the damage and report back, Brindley pored over the charred remains of the machinery, taking care to examine it from every angle even if it meant getting covered in soot. He then started to remove the damaged parts, laying them carefully on the grass outside. His diligence caused the superintendent of the mill, James Milner, to engage Brindley in conversation and a mutual admiration started to build.

Brindley seemed to grasp the principles of the machinery quickly, with most mills at the time being custom-built and therefore different from each other in detail if not in principle. He even offered some advice on how fire, the constant scourge in an environment of wood and friction, might be avoided in the future. So impressed was he that Milner sent word to Bennett that he wanted Brindley to take charge of the repair work, including supervision of the construction of fresh parts.

Bennett was suspicious. How could it be that this client wanted his 'bungler' to take charge? He decided to keep an eye on what was going on but, encouraged perhaps by Milner's close interest, he decided against interfering. With increasing satisfaction Brindley would have watched the pieces he had designed slot piece by piece into their allotted spaces, and the surge of pride that must have rushed through him when the whole apparatus worked, and worked well, must have been close to overwhelming.

Bennett was now at a loss, his apprentice had proved to be a revelation. If Brindley was looking for recognition from his master or his colleagues, however, he was in for a rude shock. As was the tradition, a supper and drinking session followed at the only inn thereabouts, during which Brindley came in for the usual ribbing and abuse, especially after the first drink had been followed by half a dozen or more.

James Milner, now firmly a Brindley fan, became incensed and decided to put an end to it. No details remain of what happened next, but it isn't difficult to imagine Milner standing on a table and shouting for quiet before levelling a finger at the assembled company and issuing his challenge:

'I will wager a gallon of the best ale in the house that before the lad's apprenticeship is out he will be a cleverer workman than any here', at which he paused meaningfully and turned his gaze towards Bennett, *'whether master or man!'*

★ ★ ★ ★ ★ ★ ★ ★ ★

Milner's advocacy from that moment on became both a millstone to Brindley and his making. Although it is not known if the wager was taken up, expectations had now been placed firmly upon Brindley's shoulders that he had to live up to. His journeymen colleagues would have now looked at him with an even more jaundiced eye. Either he had been lucky or he represented a real threat. Perhaps they had got him wrong? The easiest response was to up the rate of mickey-taking, with the gallon of best ale the easy butt of their jokes.

Meanwhile Milner was active on Brindley's behalf, perhaps anxious to justify the prediction he had made in his cups. Steadily, millers from the surrounding area would ask for 'the young man Brindley' when they had a problem. To rub salt into the wounds, some would even express a preference for him over Bennett. His master it seems was confounded, even asking Brindley where he had gained his knowledge. With due modesty he replied: 'It comes natural like'.

What seemed to be happening was that Brindley was applying his natural intelligence with the more practical skills he had learned in the workshop. Where he differed from both his master and the journeymen was his ability to work on a problem and come up with viable solutions. Rather than simply carrying out repairs he was offering improvements. What was more, his natural affinity with all things to do with water and the principles of hydrodynamics, a proclivity that was to define his place in history, were coming into play.

Many of the mills he was asked to work on were employing waterpower to operate their machinery. Faced with the alternatives of muscle power, whether of man or beast, wind or water, the potential and relative reliability of water was the best option for most of the larger mills emerging in the area. The trick was finding ways of best capturing this potential.

Brindley was a mill owner's delight and began the process of fulfilling Milner's prophecy. Not only did he bring the skills of a tradesman, but he also offered consultancy, often for free. Asked in to effect a repair, Brindley rarely left without offering some thoughts on how the machinery could work more effectively, with water often entering into the equation. What was more, his ideas worked, reaping extra profits for the mills he worked on.

How he did this remained a mystery to those who had worked with him during his bungling years. When he was called in to look over a problem Brindley would often simply gaze and stare at the situation he was presented with in silence. He took no notes or measurements and made no calculations. He would then usually retreat into a reverie that may well involve a spell in bed while he thought the problem through.

Although somewhat strange, this behaviour would not have seemed as outrageous to his contemporaries as it does to modern minds. Prodigious feats of memory were common in an age when literacy rates were low and knowledge was often passed down orally rather than through the written word. Given the lack of support he had received from those around him in the early days, Brindley also probably felt less obligation to explain what he was doing, challenging people to judge him by his results.

Emerging from his bed only when he was ready, Brindley would issue instructions on what was to be done, including details such as the precise dimensions of parts, which he had worked out and retained entirely in his head. If asked to explain, or worse to write down, his intentions he would become frustrated and even angry, asking for trust, which was increasingly forthcoming.

Half way through his apprenticeship, Bennett was forced to concede that Brindley was not the fool he had thought him to be and gave him more room for manoeuvre. He also began to take his role as master more seriously and on one occasion, on inspecting Brindley's work, was made to issue the criticism that the work was, if anything, too good – didn't the young man realise that they made their living making repairs? 'Firmness of work', he suggested was 'the ruin of trade'.

Rivers, water-wheels and mills of all types came to be Brindley's forte during this time. Perhaps the best example of his 'firmness of work' at this time is the paper mill at Wildboarclough in Cheshire, a small village two miles away from the workshop, nestled in a dark wooded valley alongside the River Dane. This was to consist of new machinery on the same river, developed along the lines of similar mills at Smedley on the River Irk and Throstle Nest on the River Irwell near Manchester. This was to be a big contract and Bennett himself took control, starting by going to the existing mills to get an understanding of what was required.

Unfortunately, these mills turned out to be too close to the temptations of the growing town of Manchester. Although nothing like the metropolis it was to become, barely more than a small town in fact, compared with Macclesfield at least Manchester would have offered a range and variety of inns a man like Abraham Bennett would have found hard to resist. Despite the importance of the contract Bennett spent more time drinking than he did examining the two paper mills.

Back at base he set his men to work on pieces of machinery using specifications dragged out from the depths of his no doubt befuddled brain. When these were taken to Wildboarclough they resembled parts of different jigsaws and it was clear to anyone who cared to look that the contract was on its way to disaster.

As it happened someone did take care to look, a local who knew a bit about paper mill machinery. What he saw was enough for him to retire to a local inn and vent forth his opinions on how the owner of the mill was wasting his money, describing the whole venture as 'a farce'. This opinion grew wings on the bush telegraph and found its way back to Brindley.

Brindley must have known about the Wildboarclough contract, but it would seem he was not part of the team chosen to execute it. Given his proved skills in all things to do with water this seems perverse, and there must be a suspicion that Bennett had deliberately excluded him with the intention of proving that Brindley was not the only one who could design a water-driven mill.

Bennett's workshop is now a garage attached to this house in Sutton Lane Ends.

If this was Bennett's intention he was to be proven sadly wrong. He refused either to abandon the lucrative contract or to involve his upstart apprentice, no matter how clear it became that he was in over his head. Eventually it became clear to Brindley that something had to be done and he could wait no longer. A charitable view would suggest that it was not in his interests for his master to have his reputation shredded. More likely, Brindley could not resist the opportunity to get his hands on the work.

Without fanfare he waited until the working week was over on Saturday and walked the twenty-five miles to Manchester on his own reconnaissance mission. There he got permission from the owner of Smedley Mill to inspect the mill, spending all of Sunday in his by now customary observance of the problem, silently establishing for himself how everything worked.

Meanwhile, back in Sutton, Bennett was beginning to panic. Brindley had not shown up at his lodgings in his master's house and he had convinced himself that Brindley, his once bungling apprentice but by now valued member of staff, had fled the nest. Brindley was now twenty-one, the age of legal majority, and it was more than possible that he had decided to make his fortune away from the travails of Bennett and his men. Bennett sent word to Brindley's mother and learnt that he wasn't there either. By then he must have been convinced his theory was true and wondering what he was going to do. Meanwhile, he had another problem to attend to.

Returning to the Wildboarclough site on Monday Bennett was amazed to be confronted by Brindley, coat off and sleeves rolled up working with his customary zeal. The moment when their eyes met must have been loaded with dramatic tension. It must have been clear to both that this was a moment of truth. In the end, Brindley won the staring competition. Although he hadn't any blueprint of what he was going to do, other than in his head, his enthusiasm and confidence left Bennett with little choice but to go along with whatever was in his mind. It is indicative that he chose to fall in meekly behind Brindley's plans, notwithstanding the fact that this was his apprentice telling him what to do. Effectively he was conceding defeat in the battle of wills between them.

Bennett handed the contract over to his apprentice. Parts already made were scrapped and new parts were built. The scheme was redesigned and built still within time and price and, most important of all, to the satisfaction of the owner. Significantly Brindley had developed an automatic water-wheel that continued in operation until 1952, over 200 years, a testament to the 'firmness' of his work.

Following the completion of Wildboarclough Mill a sea-change took place in the relationship between Brindley and his master. The contract, and with it his reputation, as well as his skin, had been saved by the apprentice. Bennett had no option other than to acknowledge this fact and he never tried to prove himself over his one-time bungler again.

Brindley now took over the workshop and became the *de facto* master. For young James this was probably more a recognition of practical reality rather than any cherished ambition. There is no evidence that he sought to exploit his position or to claim the credit for the Wildboarclough job, despite the considerable risks he had taken. Rather, the suspicion is that he simply took pride in a job well done.

Brindley stayed to serve out his apprenticeship and even remained past his time, maintaining his old master in respectable comfort long past the period when he needed to. When Bennett died he continued to display great loyalty to his old master, suggesting that perhaps some kind of bond had been forged between them following Wildboarclough, which may even have blossomed into a mutual respect over time. Rather than leave immediately, Brindley stayed to complete outstanding work in progress and until the final accounts had been agreed.

★ ★ ★ ★ ★ ★ ★ ★ ★ ★

With Bennett's death Brindley was faced with a stark choice. He had no capital to speak of and it is unlikely that his father could have raised any sum of significance, faced as he was with finding positions for the remainder of his children. He couldn't therefore buy the business from Bennett's widow even if this had been his wish. Neither could he return home, not that he would have seen this as an option either. His only real choice was to set up on his own, armed only with his skills, his growing reputation and his inventiveness.

He chose to do so in Leek, where at least some people might know of him. The main market town of the surrounding moorlands, Leek sat precariously on the side of a hill with a steep descent to a small river, a tributary of the Churnet. Contemporary accounts describe Leek as a 'middling sized, clean town with wide open streets and a spacious marketplace'. Importantly for Brindley the town was well supplied with water, which was seen as a major contributory factor to its being so clean.

It was 1742, Brindley was twenty-six and had a total of nine years experience, only around half of which could really be called true experience. An uncertain future awaited him. Although Leek was a reasonable choice in that at least he knew it, it was unpromising in its potential. Mainly a market town, there was little industry other than some making and dyeing of silk ribbons and a few grist mills with simple two-stone grindstones driven by streams; hardly enough to build a business on.

The alternative might have been to migrate to one of the bigger towns, but this too was fraught with danger. He would have seen parts of Manchester when researching the Wildboarclough project, and given his rural antecedents it is unlikely that the prospect of living there would have been that attractive. Towns such as Manchester were confusing places, growing in an *ad hoc* way without apparent rhyme or reason. Crime was rife, filth and faeces covered the streets and kites and hawks scavenged alongside the rats that carried the invisible killer – disease. Towns were somewhere to avoid.

Towns were also havens of drunkenness, in particular through gin abuse. The drinking of gin was soon to reach epidemic proportions in London and wasn't to be controlled until 1751. Although published five years later, Hogarth's engraving 'The Harlot's Progress' showed what could happen to the innocent abroad, with idealism ending in despair. For Brindley the pull of Manchester or even London would not have been a difficult one to resist. Besides, his work was in the countryside.

Leek it was then. For Brindley this would have been a definite homecoming, Lowe Hill being situated on the other side of town. Records show that 100 years before one of the town's blacksmiths had been a Brindley, and although this was a common enough Staffordshire name such knowledge would have been comforting. Being young and optimistic, as well as confident in his skills, the decision would have seemed a logical one. This was an entrepreneurial age, where those with good ideas could get a hearing. New inventions and technologies were beginning to emerge and held a fascination for the common man. Knowledge was beginning to feed upon itself and was generating a momentum that would result in an age of inventiveness and wonder, perhaps unparalleled until our own time.

Brindley's potential clients in Leek would be both simple folk and the new breed of nascent industrialists, with whom he had already had some contact and gained something of a reputation. Many of these were declared polymaths, taking an interest across a wide spectrum of the emerging sciences, not always drawing a distinction between them, and gathering in select clubs to share learning. Astronomy, biology, geology, medicine, engineering – all were challenging the frontiers of knowledge and waiting to be defined.

All this was fine in theory, but James Brindley had to make a living. An uncertain future awaited him in Leek, one in which he would have to live off his wits.

three

The Pull of Water

Like most small businessmen who start up on their own, Brindley found he had to do everything. Whilst today that might mean doing the photocopying, buying stamps and making your own tea, for Brindley it meant felling his own trees and cutting them up for timber, sharpening his own tools and undertaking all his own visits, often walking prestigious distances to do so. Recognising the obvious limitations of Leek, Brindley was prepared to go anywhere for work.

During his early days he could afford neither apprentices nor journeymen of his own, so he was obliged to cut, plane and file all his own materials, and from the start imposed high standards on himself and on his work. Commissions were always carried out on time and to excellent quality. This was a sound strategy for a man keen to create a reputation for himself. It also allowed him to charge premium rates for his services.

In this way he aimed his business at the growing band of early industrialists rather than the common man, and although not too proud to accept the occasional small repair job the reality was that agricultural wages were too low for local farmers to afford his standard of work. Brindley had learned some rudimentary writing skills whilst in Macclesfield and during his time at Leek he began to keep a simple journal. From this we know that he started to gain some work in fitting out silk-throwing mills and repairing corn mills.

Whilst his preference was always to work with water he turned down nothing where he felt he could make a difference. Examples of his work around this period include projects involving the draining of mines and the pumping of water as well as the smelting of iron and copper. To gain work he often returned to Macclesfield, where he had started his career, but he was also forced deeper into Cheshire and on occasion into Lancashire, travelling by horse and spending the evenings at local inns.

Throughout this time he maintained his approach of suggesting improvements where he saw them. To a large extent this became his trademark, leading to the conferment of the nickname 'The Schemer', an appendage it's easy to imagine Brindley revelling in. His inventiveness was particularly prized by the growing band of industrialists establishing pottery businesses around

The rear of the Brindley Mill, with the mill itself at work and drawing water away from the river. (Courtesy of Brian Moran, Brindley Mill)

the towns of Newcastle under Lyme, Trentham and Burslem and the challenges these offered. Along with the variety of work he gained elsewhere, these would have given his inventive brain good exercise.

Despite his growing reputation the evidence suggests that success was not instantaneous and remained fragile for some years. It took him a while to generate enough business to take on an apprentice to look after the workshop whilst he was away on his travels, looking for work for example. Even ten years later his journal still records him felling his own trees and spending a number of days cutting them up – although he was astute enough to charge his client at the time the going rate for manual labour, a relatively modest two shillings a day.

Inevitably perhaps, his lasting monument in Leek was a watermill. Quite what the pull of water was on Brindley it is difficult to divine. His formative years took place in an area where the only natural water would have been moorland streams, and the rivers around Lowe Hill and Macclesfield were modest at best. Perhaps it was more what water represented, its latent power, which attracted him? Water-wheels were popular motive engines for local mills and represented a contrivance open to refinement and improvement, another feature that would have appealed.

In 1750, at the age of thirty-four, Brindley was considering renting a workshop at Rotton Row in Burslem from a family called Wedgwood in order to be closer to the burgeoning industry and source of potential work around the potteries. It is possible that his commission to improve the corn mill down the road from his workshop in Mill Street in Leek came just as he was contemplating this move. If so, the project was to be a fitting reminder of his time in that town, involving as it did both major redirection of the River Churnet and solutions to the mechanical problems faced by the mill itself. If it was his intention to leave some kind of memorial then he succeeded, for in true Brindley fashion the mill lasted a good 200 years and since its closure has been renovated as a museum dedicated to the memory of the man who inspired it.

The Mill was commissioned by Thomas Jolliffe, a local landowner, and was to be built at the bottom of the hill whose peak was crowned by the church Brindley's great-grandmother had had herself thrown out of nearly 100 years before and where his parents were eventually to be buried. Some overlap probably occurred between his time in Leek and his *de facto* transfer to Burslem and he may well have had a workshop at the mill for a while, although the section where this would have been was demolished in a road-widening scheme in 1948.

In truth, the mill itself did not offer any particular innovations on Brindley's part, he had become quite expert in the design and building of such structures by this time. Its main significance lies in being about the only remaining example of his work in his pre-canals period. The sixteen foot oak water-wheel is powered by water from a mill-race taken from a bend in the River Churnet. In order to regulate the flow of water Brindley had to construct a stone weir, which remains today. This was a significant structure fashioned in an arc over fifty feet round and fifteen feet deep. The river upstream also had to be lined with stone for 100 yards because to build a head of water he had to raise the river level, necessitating the construction of a small bridge to an adjacent meadow.

The design of this bridge is quintessentially Brindley, its sides being overlaid with flat sleepers of protruding stone, a feature that later reoccurred in his canal bridges. The main doorway to the mill shares this Brindley trademark, along with stone 'E's either side which can also be spotted on Brindley canal bridges. Otherwise, the main distinguishing feature of the mill is the hanging truss on the uppermost floor. This was fashioned out of two mirror-image oak beams taken from a single oddly-shaped tree that it is easy to imagine Brindley cutting down himself. Use of a crooked tie-beam in this way also bears the Brindley trademark, being a simple solution and economic at the same time. A more conventional design would have added another three or four feet to the height of the roof, adding considerably to the cost. Perhaps Brindley had simply spotted the tree on his travels and seen its potential? On the upper floor Brindley's initials are carved on the wall along with those of the mill's owner, and it's tempting to speculate that these were inscribed by his own hand.

Towards the end of his time in Leek Brindley had found more and more of his time taken up by the demands of the ambitious pottery entrepreneurs to the south. Still very much an industry finding its feet, the potteries were finding it difficult to manufacture enough of the flint powder they needed to meet the growing demand for their finished ware. English pottery had recently undergone a radical move upmarket. For years it had been nothing much more than crude mud-brown earthenware, but the discovery of the benefits of flint powder as a dipping medium had allowed the development of more sophisticated goods, capable of intricate decoration and colouring. Broken up and mixed with the clay, flints had suddenly become a vital resource, without which simple white crockery, suitable for the masses and the elite alike, could not be made.

The problem was devising a means of breaking up the flint in sufficient quantities as conventional crushing was a random and dangerous business. Solving problems was Brindley's game, and 'The Schemer' was brought in by the up and coming Wedgwood brothers Thomas and John to tackle theirs. Brindley's solution was a mill to power a mechanism to grind the flint down, and the period towards the end of his time at Leek was increasingly taken up developing a range of flint mills for different potters.

Presented with a secure form of income at last, Brindley uprooted his workshop and finally rented the premises found for him by the Wedgwoods in Burslem. He was already familiar with the area as he had to pass through it on his horse to his other regular source of work, the home of his early patron Earl Gower of Trentham. Once again engaged in matters to do with water, Brindley had gained a strong reputation with the Earl in sorting out flooded mines and conducted work for him regularly over the next few years. Gower was also destined to play a larger part in his life's story but more on that later.

Brindley was in many ways fortunate to be near to this source of dynamic new industry, which suited his skills and interests perfectly. This was a time of depressed prices in the countryside and whilst this meant more disposable income for the common man, this was not the market Brindley had tipped his cap at. He was more interested in the larger scale farmers, but lower incomes meant less money to invest in new machinery, which may go some way to explaining why Brindley struggled to get his business going in Leek.

Accompanying the depressed economy was political and social instability, which would have added to a general sense of uncertainty. In 1745 the Jacobites had proved that the settlement following the Civil War might not be as permanent as those in power might have liked by marching as far south as Manchester, uncomfortably close to Brindley's home territory.

It was also difficult for those with land – and therefore money – to be sure whether the growing towns they saw emerging represented an opportunity or a threat. Old certainties were beginning to be chipped away at, and although the aristocracy still held a tight grip on power a growing sense that nothing was forever, even if it went unarticulated, might have been niggling away at the back of their minds. Even with this backdrop however, Brindley's career seemed to be finally gaining some momentum, aided in part by his own considerable efforts and increasing reputation, and in part to some occasional slices of luck.

★ ★ ★ ★ ★ ★ ★ ★ ★

One of those slices of luck occurred at a wedding party. Then, as now, weddings were occasions for great celebration, one of the few opportunities people had to really push to boat out and entertain their friends and family. Given high mortality rates, and the fact that men in particular tended to get married later in life when they had amassed the means to support a family, weddings were considerably rarer events than funerals, and weddings that involved both sets of parents of the bride and groom were even rarer still. Music, food, speeches and toasts would have been the order of the day, accompanied by elaborate ceremonies, including a general licence to kiss the bride and near-riots over procuring the bride's garter amongst the unmarried women of the party.

Precisely who was getting married on this particular occasion is unclear, but what we do know is that it was attended by the owner of a mine at Clifton, between Manchester and Bolton. This was probably the uncle of the bridegroom, John Heathcote, who we can

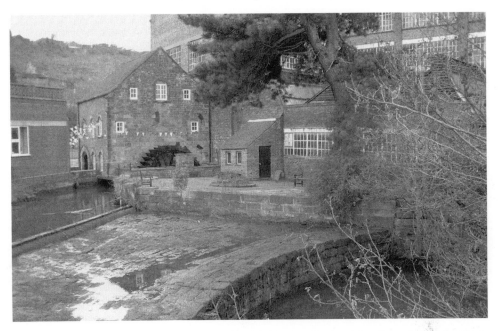

Brindley's weir for the mill in Leek is shown clearly when the mill is in operation. (Courtesy of Brian Moran, Brindley Mill)

imagine as being prosperous and ambitious, the sort of person who, whilst happy to partake of the revelry, also kept half an ear cocked to business opportunities when part of a gathering. Weddings were great places to network and to pick up the word on the turnpike and John Heathcote was probably well practised in this art.

Times remained hard for landowners and it is entirely possible that towards the end of the day a hard core of like-minded local grandees had gathered around a single table to chew the fat. That table would have been finely decorated with good linen and centrepieces full of symbolism such as eggs for fertility and corn for prosperity. The faces around the table would have been less joyous however, as each recounted their woes to a contrasting soundtrack of music and dancing, whooping and cheers.

John Heathcote's main gripe would have been the constant flooding of his Gal Pit coalmine, sometimes quite aptly known as the 'Wet Earth Colliery'. Nothing, it seemed, could stop it filling with water. All the usual techniques had been tried but had proved inadequate. Production had all but ceased, cutting off a significant source of his income.

Pressed for more information, Heathcote would have recounted the use of the traditional remedies involving chain pumps and gin wheels with giant buckets raised and lowered through the efforts of horses and mules. Although they had some effect, Heathcote and his men had quite literally been fighting against the tide. After a few nods of sympathy it seems the name of James Brindley cropped up. He was, it was suggested, something of a miracle worker when it came to anything to do with water. Perhaps Heathcote and he should meet? At this point perhaps the colliery owner looked up and pressed for more information and heard of some of the feats accomplished by this young man. All would have agreed that a meeting would indeed be a good idea – anything was worth a go.

At the meeting that followed, Heathcote was able to give a full exposition of the problem, right down to a description of the rock strata beneath the ground and how it sloped. Brindley, as was his habit, would have listened and contemplated the facts, remaining silent, disarmingly so, while he thought. Heathcote it seems gave him the space he needed, perhaps lighting up a pipe whilst he waited. And waited. And waited.

Eventually a smile began to thaw the serious look on Brindley's face and he began to explain his proposed solution. It was novel, it was daring, and it was elegant. Best of all it looked as if it made economic sense and Heathcote was unable to see a flaw in his argument. Perhaps Heathcote was desperate, or perhaps Brindley was simply utterly convincing. Whichever the truth, he was commissioned on the spot.

After a period of thorough preparation, work started on Brindley's plan. Part of what made it so convincing was its boldness. Brindley proposed a series of tunnels designed to use the power of the adjacent River Irwell, a river that was later to feature in both his dreams and his nightmares, and the fact that it was tidal, to operate a giant water-wheel thirty feet in diameter hidden inside the coal mine, which in turn operated a pump. Water pulled up by the pump was then sent through another tunnel and subsequently out of the mine.

As with his mill project in Leek, he also proposed to construct a weir to channel the river's power to suit his needs. The tunnel at the north side of the weir was 600 yards long and driven through first shale and then sandstone, with parts of it bricked up. Another tunnel, or more of a shaft, fifty-three feet long was also part of the scheme, as was a horizontal tunnel 220 feet long to take the water away. Water pumped out from the mine was then directed back into the Irwell through a tailrace tunnel.

Although a grand design, Brindley was able to make the project viable by offering to do it at rock bottom prices. Once again, we see Brindley absorbed by the challenge more than the prospect of material gain. Entries in his notebook suggest that he himself worked for a labourer's wage of two shillings a day, a rate that hardly reflected his intellectual contribution. He also used only a small team, armed simply with hammers and chisels to dig the tunnels, and using only basic candles for light. Digging the tunnels would have been a wet, claustrophobic and thankless task, but provided valuable experience for some of his later triumphs.

Speed, it seemed, was also sacrificed for the sake of economy, or possibly simply to allow Heathcote the means to finance the project over time. In the end the whole scheme took four years to complete, which demonstrates a remarkable act of faith on the part of the mine owner. It was faith that was to be amply justified.

When the scheme was finished in 1756 the water went where it should, the wheel turned as predicted and the mine was duly pumped dry of water. Work recommenced at the coalface and seams long thought drowned were reopened. Once again, Brindley's 'firmness of work' has been demonstrated by history, with the wheel lasting over 100 years and the tunnels even longer, production eventually ceasing in 1928. In Brindley's day the pit was soon recording an income of £6,200 a year, providing work for 150 men. Although there must have been times when he had had his doubts, in hiring Brindley John Heathcote had made one of the best business decisions of his life.

Given the fact that the drop in water from the top of the weir to the underground wheel was thirty-five feet, and that water was lifted from a depth of over 150 feet, in solving the Wet

Earth Colliery problem Brindley was to earn another sobriquet: 'The Man Who Made Water Run Uphill'. There was, it seemed, no man like him when it came to mastering water.

From this period on Brindley's business kicked up a gear. News of the Wet Earth Colliery project no doubt helped, but managing this only took up some of his time. Once the project was in train he moved to more of a supervisory role, releasing time to take up other commissions. His success with the corn mill at Leek, for example, had led to calls to exercise his skills on projects at Wheelock, Codan, Ashbourne, Marchant Brooks and Trentham.

Pockets of local manufacturing were also becoming more common around this time, with men of capital becoming slightly more daring in how they invested their funds. Confidence was beginning to flow back into the economy but, as it remains today, this was a slow process. As for the wider case for investing in manufacturing over farming, well this was one where the jury was still out.

A good example of this growing confidence arose in Congleton, half way between Leek and Macclesfield, where in 1755 a Mr Gilbert, a London-based entrepreneur, engaged a group of local businessmen and landowners in an ambitious plan to capitalise on local expertise in making silk for buttons. This activity, almost by definition, had leant itself to small-scale production, either in individual houses or small workshops. His daring scheme was to create a facility large enough to generate silk in bulk to supply the growing demand for such consumer goods in London and beyond.

The prescience of these men was remarkable. Already Congleton, along with Macclesfield, was making a name for itself as an industrial centre. Along with silk buttons the town had become a thriving centre for glove and shoelace manufacture, with leather laces finished with silver points known as Congleton Points. Such specialisation and movement away from cottage-based manufacture to factories was a symptom of an increasingly sophisticated economy, but remained the exception rather than the rule. Men prepared to back their ideas with money were still the trailblazers.

There had been investment in mills in the area since 1744, when Italian silk-throwing machinery had been installed, and, two years before Gilbert's scheme, John Claydon of Stockport had built a mill for water-powered silk throwing at a cost in excess of £5,000. This forerunner of the modern factory had seventy-five winding engines performing 32,850 movements – and that excluded the cleaning engines.

The entrepreneurs of Congleton were clearly no fools, and although Brindley's reputation was good it had yet to reach the stage where it carried all before it. Gilbert and his men decided to split responsibility for the work in order to cover their bets, placing overall control into the hands of a superintendent called Johnson. Brindley's role was to design and deliver the main water-wheel, where it was felt his main expertise lay, along with some of the more basic parts of the mechanism.

Although a decent commission, it is likely that Brindley would have been slightly put out by the fact that Johnson, being a master joiner and millwright, was entrusted with the smaller wheel and more complex parts of the machinery. This was of course a recipe for disaster. Johnson gave Brindley only verbal instructions and kept him well away from the models of the machinery he was using as his guide. Brindley was effectively working in the dark.

Things soon went badly wrong, with parts made by the two men not fitting together and a growing sense of unease beginning to ferment amongst the financiers behind the project. At

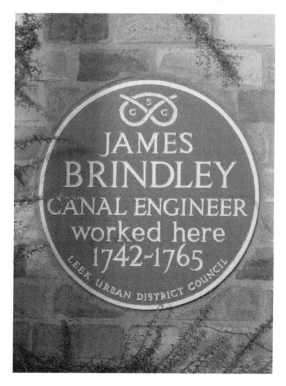

Brindley's life is recorded by this plaque over the mill in Leek. (Courtesy of Brian Moran, Brindley Mill)

first Johnson's assurances that everything was alright were taken at face value, but after a series of obvious failures even he had to admit that he wasn't up to the task.

Once again Brindley found himself in the position of having to clear up the mistakes of a supposed superior. As at Wildboarclough the project faced ruin. The components put together so far were little better than a child's incomplete puzzle. A semblance of panic began to gather amongst the men behind the project. It seemed that Brindley was their only hope, but was he up to the task? The balance of risk was finely pitched. Should they cut their losses or invest everything on this relatively unknown, unlettered and occasionally, to their eyes and ears, uncouth man? He seemed confident enough and had a lot about him but …

Brindley moved the debate forward by asking to see the models that had so far been denied to him. Johnson, in a fit of pique, refused; claiming that as a 'common millwright' Brindley was not fit to see his plans. Brindley's natural talent it seems was capable of stirring up considerable professional jealousy. Exasperated sighs must have followed from all involved. For many Johnson's behaviour confirmed deeper inadequacies. Brindley turned the problem on its head and asked exactly what it was the would-be proprietors wanted to achieve? On being told, he offered to deliver the machinery they needed, but with one proviso: that he be allowed to do it his way, without outside interference.

Brindley asked for trust, and was given it. In truth, the men behind the mill probably had little choice, but we can only assume that they took soundings on Brindley's ability to deliver before granting him his wishes. This was a big project, taking Brindley into new territory. The would-be proprietors were right to suppose that he had little experience in the minutiae of working machinery, his reputation to date had mainly been as a big ideas man, operating on a grand scale, fording rivers and digging tunnels, not the intricate and often delicate workings of a silk mill.

To Brindley however, this was simply a matter of scale. The principles of problem solving and engineering were the same. What was more he had spent a great deal of his working life around mills. He had exercised his acute powers of observation on how they worked and how they could be improved. It is entirely likely that he had been looking for an opportunity like this for some time.

He duly delivered. The power was provided by the customary water-wheel, something that would have been almost second nature to him by then. The clever bit was how he used that power. Brindley introduced a number of refinements to conventional milling machinery that simply overwhelmed his clients. He adapted lifts to each set of rollers and swifts, which meant that the silk could be wound onto their bobbins evenly rather than in a wreath, as was conventional practice.

He also arranged the shafting of the mill so that parts of it could be shut down without having to pause the whole operation. Although this may seem an obvious thing to do, no one had done it before and the improvements this one change made to productivity were on their own enough to reward his clients' faith. There was more though. He even manufactured the machinery that in turn produced the cogs that were such an integral part of the mill's workings. Previously each had been made by hand. In this way their quality was standardised and inconsistency and breakdowns were cut at a stroke. Again, no one had gone this far before. The Congleton Silk Mill became a model of its type.

Having established such a niche, a modern-day adviser would direct such an inventor to capitalise on his reputation by repeating his successes. Not so Brindley. His satisfaction came from fresh challenges, and there was no shortage of those.

★ ★ ★ ★ ★ ★ ★ ★ ★ ★

During this time Brindley's journals see him raising his charges, from two shillings a day at the beginning of the Congleton project to two shillings and six pence a year later and three shillings a day a couple of years after that. Around that time a common labourer could hope to earn around a shilling a day, but Brindley had a workshop and workers to keep, so even with this rise he was not on course to becoming a rich man. By way of comparison, assuming he worked six days a week for fifty weeks a year, but was only able to charge for two-thirds of these, his annual income would be £30. Estimates for other trades for this period suggest that this would equate to a low-earning freehold farmer or a skilled carpenter or blacksmith.

Perhaps Brindley had reached the point where he had proven his talent and it was time to reap some material gain from it? Like any good modern-day professional he seemed to have understood that his day rate was just one way of securing income. His journals show him becoming meticulous in recording his expenses, such as those incurred for his horse (the eighteenth century equivalent of charging for mileage) and for overnight stops at inns (travel and subsistence). We also find him increasingly willing to be used as a consultant rather than labourer and charging accordingly. This was an age when there was no shortage of people coming up with good ideas and seeking a second opinion before committing themselves to expenditure. This Brindley was pleased to provide – at a price. Records of cutting down his own trees do not feature at this time.

By now Brindley had turned forty. He had established himself and weathered the bad times. He remained unmarried, although this was not a totally unusual state at his age, but seemed content to satisfy his spirit through a constant stream of fresh challenges. He was riding the wave of his talent and of the opportunities of the period.

At the same time he was becoming more conscious of his age. Then, perhaps more than now, turning forty was a significant milestone. His journals see him becoming more preoccupied with his health, jotting down remedies he picked up on his travels for common complaints for future reference. These ranged from recipes for hot poultices to treat a bad back through to drinking your own warm urine for ague or fevers. Anything, it would seem, to avoid the ministrations of the medical profession.

One of the challenges he was to return to at this time was to refine the processes for grinding flint for the by now burgeoning pottery trade. Although he had worked on this before, the demand for flint powder was now growing almost exponentially and the whole process needed a re-think. So it was that in 1757 we find Brindley being engaged by the Tunstall potter Thomas Baddeley – to whom, incidentally, he charged different rates for different tasks ranging from two and six to four shillings a day.

As was by now his instinct, Brindley employed waterpower to crank up the power of existing flint mills. At Baddeley's mill he again constructed the water-wheel underground, ensuring a constant supply of water to it through a 200 yard long channel. With ever an eye to efficiency, the buckets on the wheel were covered in leather to prevent seepage. The wheel powered both a set of stampers, to ground the flints to powder, as well as a pump to drain the adjacent coal mine, a particularly elegant solution that must have appealed to him.

During this period Brindley was fully employed, rushing around on a variety of projects often linked to mills and water, as well as the occasional repair work. His journals tell us that he was not afraid to sub-contract elements of his projects, but give no evidence of collaborations with like-minded professionals. Brindley was still his own man.

During this spell in the potteries it was inevitable that he should re-establish contact with Thomas and John Wedgwood, uncles to the ultimately more famous Josiah, but at that time more-established names in the pottery business. They too were preoccupied with the problem of flint grinding and came to Brindley for assistance. What they had in mind however was a windmill, to power pumps that brought water up from a well rather than a river, as well as the stampers. This was to be constructed at The Jenkins, on a hill outside Burslem. This application of a fresh source of nature's abundant energy must have appealed to Brindley, whose childhood would have been marked by memories of the howling winds of Derbyshire.

Both the Wedgwoods and Brindley had become increasingly concerned about the effect of flint dust on those working near the grinders and for Brindley the answer was obvious: grind the flints under water. His solution involved building a large round vat, a yard or so deep, through the centre of which ran the vertical shaft of the windmill. This was filled with a particularly hard type of flint called chert, that was plentiful around Bakewell in Derbyshire, and ground to dust by four large stones placed at right angles inside the vat.

The original eighteenth century tentering gear at the Brindley Mill in Leek, showing an oak 'bridge tree' resting on a brayer, both of which are pivoted. (Courtesy of Brian Moran, Brindley Mill)

The theory at least was sound. Less so were the calculations that had gone into the windmill itself. Although the idea of setting the mill off on a particularly windy day might have seemed like a good one at the time, events proved otherwise. With no doubt a small crowd gathered to witness the power of the windmill in action – the sails and gearing were said to be unusually large and impressive – disaster struck as the wind caught the sails, ripping them at first and then stripping them from the mill.

With the crowd dashing for cover inside the mill, the noise up above must have been terrifying as the howling wind wrought its damage and the creaking and crashing of the machinery echoed within the stone walls. It is entirely possible that it was experiences such as these that later translated into Brindley's apparent nervousness on the day of the opening of the Barton Aqueduct.

A blot upon the Brindley copybook this might have been, but the sails were fixed and the mill performed efficiently for years, in so doing instigating a fast, safe and efficient new process for a common problem. Disaster was turned into triumph, and Brindley subsequently gained a number of commissions for similar devices.

This experimentation with wind power is interesting, for it was around this time that Brindley seemed to display a need for fresh challenges. That this was an age of increasing innovation cannot be disputed. New wonders were appearing all the time, often little more than notions or ideas that a fertile mind like Brindley's could pick up and run with, refining, improving and making them more efficient along the way.

One of the most significant of these developments was steam power. The pull of steam must have been irresistible to Brindley, for what is steam other than water under pressure, the power of water multiplied manifold; a quantum leap away from the limitations of the traditional power sources of man, beast, wind and water.

What is more, the applications of steam engines since their invention by Newcomen nearly half a century before had been limited to pumping out mines. Here was the power source of the future, one not dependent upon nature, but one that could be controlled and harnessed. It was the ideal opportunity for an inventive man entering his early forties to cement his reputation and satiate his thirst for challenge.

Brindley journeyed to Wolverhampton in the Black Country to satisfy his curiosity. There he saw one of Newcomen's engines and studied it with his usual intensity. Immediately his mind began to consider ways in which the operation of the principle of steam power could be improved. His greatest concern was the efficiency of the device. Its consumption of coal made it prohibitively expensive, except in places where coal was plentiful or, as at a mine head, where it was a by-product of the process involved.

He got his chance with a commission to build a steam engine for the Broad family in the potteries. This seemed to be reasonably successful as he was commissioned to do another by the family. As was his way, having mastered the basic idea, Brindley took this opportunity to experiment with improvements. His first instinct was to substitute wood for iron wherever possible, starting with the cylinders and even including the construction of wooden chains. When this failed he conceded that the cylinders needed to be made of iron, but that they could be insulated with wood, with a wood ash layer in between.

This new challenge reinvigorated Brindley. He rushed around, supervising everything from the making of the boilerplates and pipes at a local ironworks to even felling his own trees again. Maybe this was a kind of therapy while he waited for the iron components to be completed? Maybe it was to save money? Maybe he had deliberately under-quoted in order to get the work? Whatever the reasons, his journals again record him spending three-and-a-half days to fell a big tree for the project.

A measure of his obsession during this period was the sheer volume of time he devoted to the Fenton project. Five days to get the 'great lever fixed', a full thirty-nine days to put the boiler together and thirteen days to get the pit prepared. This was at a time when he was still working with the Wedgwoods, as well as continuing his millwork and doing the occasional repair job such as overhauling some pumps for Earl Gower of Trentham.

After a year's hard graft the engine was ready, but if he was expecting his usual triumph, Brindley was to be disappointed. Although it worked, it did so only intermittently. Time after time he had to return to it to get it going again, baby-sitting it as it coughed and belched and ultimately wheezed to a stop. Months later he was still returning to it trying to get it to work. For the first time since the early days of his apprenticeship he was faced with something that was defying his talents.

The frustration for Brindley, let alone the probable exasperation of his client, must have been immense. The most charitable interpretation of the conclusion of this episode is that Brindley got the engine to work after a fashion, and even then by only going back on some of his proposed innovations. At best this engine was a qualified success and in March 1758 he was paid over £70 in settlement, a not inconsiderable sum given this represented twice his

The breast-shot waterwheel with oak arms and blades at the Brindley Mill, although the rims and axle are nineteenth-century cast iron. (Courtesy of Brian Moran, Brindley Mill)

probable annual salary, but this sum would have included materials and it is not inconceivable that Brindley had pushed himself into debt to complete the work. Whether to vent his frustration or in celebration, shortly afterwards his journals record a drinking spree, a decidedly uncharacteristic response from Brindley, during which he spent a whole eighteen pence.

Understandably a brief rest from steam ensued, with Brindley returning to the problem of flint mills. Through the spring and summer of 1758 however, Brindley was back working on 'a new invention' for a Mr Talbot and a Mr Griffiths, giving the occasional burst of activity to the project. Throughout his career though, Brindley had used failure as an opportunity to learn, and so it was again here. On Boxing Day 1758 he duly filed a patent for a steam engine whose boiler would be made of brick or stone arched over, with a cast iron stove fixed within the boiler. The chains were still made of wood, as were the pumps, which would be staved together.

This was in effect Brindley's gambit in the evolving debate over how a steam engine should best be constructed, although eventually fundamental flaws were exposed in this design. His interest in the subject continued for a while, with further commissions for steam engines the following year, although how successful these were we don't know, and fully five years later he was involved in construction of an all-iron steam engine for the Walker Colliery in Newcastle under Lyme, determined perhaps to work through the problem to his own satisfaction. This was reasonably successful and, along with a further engine at Worsley mine, seems to have been his final statement on the matter, giving him the chance to retire from the field with some grace. His enthusiasm seemed to wane and steam's cudgels were picked up more comprehensively by others, notably James Watt.

A different challenge, one perhaps more in line with his special talents, was about to come his way. At first this seemed like a distraction, but eventually it was to take over his life and make his name. Shortly before the conclusion of the Fenton engine episode, in February 1758, he had been engaged by the Earl of Gower and Lord Anson to conduct a survey to explore the potential of an artificial waterway sweeping across the backbone of the country to link the two great rivers of the Trent and the Mersey. More specifically, he was asked to investigate the feasibility of a canal linking Lichfield in Staffordshire and Burton on Trent as part of the more major scheme.

This was a perfectly logical thing to ask him to do, given his natural bent towards problem solving and his understanding of geology and most of all of water dynamics. Journal entries at this time simply record this activity without comment, and it is possible that he had taken the work as much for the money as for the challenge. Whatever his motivation, Brindley was happy to conclude for his masters that such an enterprise was perfectly possible, although the costs attached would make investment prohibitive.

And there it was left.

four

Patrons and Personalities

Most of us are lucky if during our lives we come across one significant personality, a patron, a mentor or Svengali, capable of changing our outlook or direction through the sheer force of their personality. James Brindley was lucky enough to have at least three. Two have already been mentioned in this narrative, the third has yet to take his bow.

Two of Brindley's patrons were from the highest echelons of British nobility; the other was to become a founding member and leading light of the new aristocracy of industrialists. That Brindley could be introduced to, influenced by and at times almost adopted by these men is a testament to both his talent and the relative social fluidity of the time.

It is easy to over-state the case for this fluidity in Georgian England, but the pot of change was coming rapidly to the boil, even if the ingredients inside were still relatively raw. Money still spoke, the King remained at the centre of court, and it would have been inconceivable for a labouring peasant to dream of even owning his own home. At the micro-scale there were often very fine distinctions within social strands. A second footman would be highly aware of the difference between himself and a first footman. Which deck a sailor slept on said everything about his position within the maritime pecking order.

That said there was a remarkable level of equality within society. Peers of the realm could be, and indeed were, hanged for murder along with common men. They waited their turn in the turnpike queue and might sup at the local inn rubbing shoulders with their estate workers.

Death rates amongst all classes were high, which meant that anyone's life could be turned upside-down suddenly and without warning, regardless of rank. Most people knew of someone who had experienced a rapid change in circumstances, even if they were a friend of a friend. After all, Brindley's family had themselves undergone something of a social transformation, even if in their case it represented more of a return to a position once held and subsequently lost. People accepted the possibility of change and society had to find ways of adapting to meet this possibility.

Distinctions, whether on the grand or minor scale, were not cast in stone, they could be challenged and beaten. Unlike most of the rest of Europe, England was not a rigid society.

A fledgling middle class – the 'middling sort' – was emerging, who in themselves were challenging traditional distinctions by creating a new mix of money and birth. So long as he dressed correctly and learnt how to behave a new entrant to this class could be accepted by his peers, as well as those with more established wealth, with relative ease; even if total acceptance took a bit longer. In time, this group would grow in both size and economic importance at the same time creating and satisfying a new consumerism through their efforts.

A good example of this was Josiah Wedgwood, one of the three significant personalities in Brindley's life. Like Brindley, Josiah Wedgwood was born into a highly modest, but not peasant, family. Today the name Wedgwood is synonymous with ceramics, and at the time of his birth Josiah's family were already in the trade working in the area around Stoke on Trent we now call the 'Potteries'. At the time however, Stoke was only one of many areas with a preponderance of potters, a cluster more than an industrial area.

Like those around him, Josiah's father operated with a single kiln or potbank attached to his house. The goods he produced were low grade, being rough, uneven and unattractive. It would have been a hard way to make a living and as soon as was practicable Josiah was sent to work for his slightly more successful uncle. He was eight years old at the time. As if to illustrate the precariousness and random nature of eighteenth century life, shortly after this happened his father died unexpectedly, and the kiln was left to his eldest son William. Josiah was left £20 in his father's will, a reasonable sum but not really enough to establish a new life on.

Things got worse when, aged only fourteen and recently apprenticed to his brother Thomas, Josiah fell victim to an epidemic of smallpox running through the country. Although he survived the disease his right leg became so badly infected that he couldn't apply any pressure to it and had to keep it rested on a stool. This infection was to prove the bane of his life, spreading to his knee and, later in life, becoming so rotten that he had to resort to the drastic and risky expedient of amputation. Given the technology of the time, he needed his leg to power the potter's wheel, so without it he couldn't pursue the family business. It would have been reasonable for him at this stage to have wondered what alternative the future had in store for him.

Around that period the pottery industry was facing particularly difficult times. The organised pottery trade in the Orient had been flooding European markets with cheap porcelain for decades and a few potteries had started to fight back. More highly organised than the scattered potbanks of Stoke, these early factories threatened to wipe out the small one-man bands. Although their markets were different, few common men could, or even wanted to, own delicate porcelain. This new ware raised expectations, however. By comparison, the lumpen dark brown earthenware of Stoke looked increasingly cheap and nasty.

Josiah must have been aware of this, as he spent some of his enforced idleness researching alternatives, turning his attention not only to the materials used in traditional Stoke pottery but also its glazes, colours and shapes. Unable to turn a wheel, he experimented, whilst at the same time learning his trade. At the age of nineteen, as his apprenticeship ended, his brother let him go. Although with hindsight it is easy to see this as a massive error of judgement, Josiah couldn't have represented much of a prospect. A young cripple with ideas above his station, it is likely that Thomas was only too pleased to see the back of him, his familial duties fulfilled.

Fortunately for Josiah, others were happier to embrace this young upstart. After a year working in partnership with two other potters at Cliff Bank in Stoke, the young Wedgwood

The Duke of Bridgewater in his later
years, by which time he had become one
of the richest men in England. (Courtesy
of Manchester Central Library)

entered an agreement with Thomas Whieldon, a master potter with one of the largest potteries in Staffordshire. Whieldon was open to new ideas and had started to produce salt-glazed earthenwares and even 'Creamwares', so called because of their colour.

Like Brindley, Wedgwood was an inveterate experimenter, which may explain why they got on so well when they finally met. Working with Whieldon he introduced new and vibrant colours and effects, including a mottled 'tortoiseshell' ware. Putting his ideas into action he also worked with Whieldon to produce items that look strangely kitsch to modern eyes, such as pottery in the shape of cauliflowers, melons and pineapples, but were all the rage in the mid-seventeenth century.

In 1759, just as Brindley was about to enter the most significant phase of his life, Wedgwood set up on his own. Operating out of a modest house he manufactured niche products such as knife handles, boxes and trinkets, although the suspicion has to be that he did this as much to bring in a wage as for the aesthetic value he was creating, as he spent increasing amounts of his time on further experimentation. One of his ideas, simple enough to us now, was to prove decisive. He applied the principles of the division of labour to his works, thereby reducing costs and increasing quality.

During this time the relationship between Wedgwood and Brindley was almost certainly strictly on a business level, acquaintances rather than friends. This was the sort of relationship that might be acknowledged by a nod towards each other if they met on the street, although it was just as likely that both would have walked with their heads deep in contemplation and would have missed each other.

Brindley's work to date had been for Thomas and John Wedgwood, Josiah's uncles, although they undoubtedly came into increasing contact. Brindley's workshop in Burslem would have been very close to Wedgwood's own works and word would have passed of each other's achievements. In time their relationship might have become more self-supporting, reinforcing rather than challenging each other's triumphs. They were kindred spirits in an exciting age. By the end of the 1750s both Brindley and Wedgwood had established a reputation in their respective fields, and both stood on the brink of their golden years.

Like Brindley, Wedgwood was a perfectionist. Later in life he would wander his factories seeking out goods that fell below his very high standards. If he found any rejects he would unscrew his wooden leg and smash the offending articles to smithereens. Like Brindley, Wedgwood was always interested in better ways of doing things and applied this enthusiasm to the transformation of his chosen field. Like Brindley, his genius was the classic combination of inspiration and perspiration, breakthroughs founded on relentless trial and error and the confidence to push at boundaries. It has been estimated that the blue and white Jasperware that most associate the Wedgwood name with today required over 5,000 experiments before it was ready.

Wedgwood's rise and rise was driven largely by his early grasp of the principles of marketing. He understood the need to influence perceptions in the marketplace and to create demand. He gained patronage from both his own Queen and the Queen of Russia, producing extravagant sets of crockery, even if it meant doing so at a loss. He opened showrooms in London to literally show off his ideas and he experimented relentlessly with new designs and techniques, understanding absolutely the advantage of being the first to create a market.

Like Brindley, Wedgwood had come up the hard way. Neither forgot their humble roots, but Wedgwood's growing wealth put him in a position to do something about it. Perhaps the greatest manifestation of this was his Etruria works, built in a rural setting when mining subsidence threatened his old works, with the aim of providing a healthy working and living environment for his employees. By this time Wedgwood was into mass production for a mass market that he had had a large part in creating.

In later life Wedgwood was also an ardent supporter of those campaigning for the abolition of the slave trade as well as universal male suffrage, and he also became a Unitarian. As he grew more successful he took his friend Brindley under his wing, introducing him to some of the great thinkers whose circle he had entered, such as the illustrious physician Erasmus Darwin (later grandfather to Charles Darwin) who in turn formed a close bond. He also introduced him to other friends from the influential Lunar Club, that met monthly to discuss everything from philosophy to geology, although how Brindley, who articulated himself best through doing rather than talking, coped is not recorded. What we do know is that he didn't become a member.

But despite all his friends, connections and growing wealth there was one thing Wedgwood couldn't do, and that was unblock the calcified transport network that was proving to be a major constraint upon further expansion of his business. Mass production required mass distribution and the means didn't exist to satisfy this need. It was all very well being innovative, but without a decent transport infrastructure Wedgwood was unlikely to realise the national or indeed international potential of his goods.

The potteries of Staffordshire, of which there were around 130 by the middle of the century, had to be supplied by trains of mules plodding discordantly along unmade roads, in practice little more than ancient cattle runs, with heavy sacks of clay slumped across their backs. To make matters worse, finished ware had to leave the same way, vulnerable to the odd slip as the mules or their leaders fell into a pothole, or to thieves or the weather. Breakages accounted for as much as half the average load by the time these trains reached their destinations.

It was in solving this problem that the two friends became united in a common purpose, but that forms a future part of our story. In the meantime, Wedgwood was confined to the unsatisfactory expedient of lobbying for turnpike roads, addressing a meeting at Newcastle under Lyme Town Hall in 1763 in terms so passionate that he got his way. In time this and other turnpikes would see the 'Potteries', as they could now be legitimately called, forge some kind of link with London and, crucially, with the seaports of Liverpool and Chester.

It was in this lobbying for turnpikes that we come across the second of the significant personalities in Brindley's life, for Wedgwood, still only 33, was astute enough to enlist the support of Lord Gower of Trentham, local landowner and Member of Parliament for Staffordshire, in steering the Turnpike Bill through Parliament.

Granville Leveson-Gower was about as noble as they come. Like all of the patrons featured here he was younger than Brindley, in this case by five years. His father had been Sir John Leveson, who had been created Earl Gower in 1746, a title Granville inherited in 1754. During a long and distinguished career in politics, the Earl was to hold the posts of Lord Privy Seal, Lord of the Admiralty and Lord Chamberlain to the King, as well as being the Member of Parliament for three different constituencies, including Staffordshire and Westminster. As a reward for all this activity he was also made a Knight of the Garter in 1771 and created the First Marquess of Stafford in 1786.

In between all this activity Gower found time to get closely involved in one of his many estates, that at Trentham, outside Stoke on Trent. Although not short of cash, his political career is probably a good illustration of his wider ambition. Like Brindley's third patron he felt no embarrassment in getting personally involved in finding ways of optimising income from his lands, even if this meant dirtying his hands with matters of trade.

It was in this capacity that he is important to this story. As we have already seen, Lord Gower was one of the first to spot Brindley's talents and engaged him on a number of works, usually to do with his mines. This was during a phase of his career when steady work from a patron would have been a useful asset. Brindley's journals include a number of references to work for Gower including the pumping out of mines and the fixing of mills. It was also Gower who insisted that Brindley got involved in the early survey for the proposed canal to link the Trent and Mersey rivers.

What differentiates a patron from a client however, is his ability to supply more than simply work, and in this Gower was amply equipped. In 1748, aged only 24, Gower married his second wife, his first marriage having lasted less than six months. Critically this was to Louisa Egerton, sister to Francis Egerton, the third Duke of Bridgewater and Brindley's third great patron. Lord Gower was therefore the Duke's brother in law and the two are known to have spent a lot of time together.

As we have seen, Gower was also friendly with Josiah Wedgwood and this friendship, and mutual respect for Brindley, was to prove crucial in the later phase of Brindley's career. Critically, Gower's employee and land agent was Thomas Gilbert, who was older brother to John Gilbert, the Duke's own agent, and it is reasonable to assume that this was more than mere coincidence given the familial ties between them.

James Brindley in his later years with his trademark level. (Courtesy of Manchester Central Library)

Francis Egerton should never really have become a Duke. His nearest and dearest didn't even pin much hope on his surviving to adulthood and as such invested very little emotional or intellectual energy into him. As is often the way with men who become great, his early life was defined by a series of unplanned events, with destiny apparently driving his passage into history.

Francis was born in 1736, the son of Scroop Egerton, then Earl of Bridgewater and a successful player in Court politics in the late Stuart and early Georgian period, so successful in fact that he was created the first Duke of Bridgewater in 1720. Following the death of his first wife, Scroop chose one of the great English families, the Russells, for his second and had five sons in relatively quick succession by Lady Rachel Russell, the last of which was Francis.

Having delivered of an heir and a number of spares, it is easy to see how Francis, given the role of women of standing at the time, received little in the way of parental affection, especially as he was a sickly child and perceived as something of the runt of the litter. He was also seen as being a bit dim, and measures were put in train for the succession should, heaven forfend, he should ever be in a position to inherit the title. Fortunately for British history these steps were never taken any further.

Hope of any fatherly attention ended when Scroop died when his youngest son was only nine. Any expectation that the slack might be taken up by his mother was dashed when she married Sir Richard Lyttleton a year later and adopted an effervescent lifestyle in London's increasingly busy social circles. Amongst this busy whirl there was no place for Francis. Although easy to condemn now, this behaviour would have been perfectly normal for the times and Francis was left pretty much to his own devices under a succession of tutors.

On his father's death the title passed to his eldest brother John, but his incumbency was to be short when he in turn died of consumption aged only 21, unmarried and therefore without heirs. In the meantime the unthinkable had come to pass as one by one all of Francis' other brothers also died. With the spares all used up he was left the only remaining heir. Thus, aged only twelve, Francis, the ailing and apparently somewhat backward youngest son of an ancient family, became the third Duke of Bridgewater.

At this point his mother was forced to pay him some attention. Up until then his education had all but been ignored on the grounds that he was unlikely to live to make much use of it. As such there was a lot of ground to catch up. Against all the odds, it seemed that of all her children the ailing Francis looked like he was going to make it. With admirable clarity the decision was made to appoint the Duke of Bedford and Lord Trentham (later Lord Gower!) as his joint guardians, thus absolving responsibility for the child and keeping him out of the way. As soon as he was old enough, aged only seventeen, they in turn sent Francis abroad on the fashionable Grand Tour of Europe with a classical scholar called Robert Wood.

This event can quite reasonably be seen as revealing for the young Duke. From being somewhat cloistered away for most of his life the variety and delights of the continent were revealed to him, feeding his until then somewhat undernourished brain. The experience must have been overwhelming, taking in as it did the usual trophies of Paris, Florence and Rome. The Duke and Wood were an ill-matched pair though and relations between them were rarely good. Francis did what was expected of him and acquired various works of art, but these were said to have remained in their packing cases until his death. What really grabbed his attention it seems were some of the engineering achievements they passed, and Francis had to pester his reluctant tutor to return to some of them for a second look.

His duty discharged, Wood left, later to become an Under-Secretary of State, and Francis duly entered society. What a prospect! Aged only twenty he was a rich, titled young man with just enough knowledge to hold a conversation in polite society and nothing much to do. The temptation to enter the giddy social round was irresistible and he took to it with relish.

Parties and balls followed, and the Duke indulged a passion for horse-racing, occasionally riding himself, at times lucky not to kill himself, as he was still a light man with nothing much to him. Young and impressionable, the Duke had until then been largely starved of female company. His name became linked to young beauties, in particular that of Elizabeth Gunning, considered to be the most beautiful woman in London at the time. One of two sisters, these adventuresses had come to London from Ireland on the marriage trail, their beauty their prime assets as their family had little money.

Very quickly both had succeeded in their quest, Elizabeth accepting the hand of the Duke of Hamilton in 1752 and her sister Maria that of the Earl of Coventry. The fairy tale didn't end there though, as the Duke died shortly afterwards, placing Elizabeth in the role of merry widow with a long string of admirers, even lovers. Francis knew what he wanted and went after it. He had fallen hopelessly for the widow. His attentions were in time first acknowledged and then encouraged and, as soon as he was old enough, he proposed and was accepted.

His life seemed now to be mapped out, and a joyous prospect it must have seemed, when another one of those quirks of fate that defined both his and Brindley's story took place. Rumours reached the Duke's ear that Elizabeth's sister Maria was up to no good, cheating on her husband. It is possible that some of the society gossips had had enough of these upstart girls and had decided to put them in their place, who knows? Whatever the truth, the effect was that Francis felt compelled to demand of his fiancée that she would have to break off all contact with her sister if the marriage was to go ahead.

Together, the sisters had gone a long way and must have felt strong bonds. This was a heavy demand from the Duke but he held firm on it. Perhaps it was his relative lack of worldliness that made him stick to his guns, for rumours without proof could surely have been tolerated given his reported love for his chosen bride, but in the end his demand was enough to break the engagement. It cannot be ruled out that through her behaviour Elizabeth forced the Duke to adopt the position he did, for shortly after she broke the Duke's heart she married the Duke of Argyle, a slightly better prospect.

As if to show that there were no hard feelings Francis threw the happy couple a ball, but this was to be his swansong on the London circuit. There can be little doubt that he had been left bereft by the whole affair with Elizabeth, as straight after the ball he retreated from society, eschewing the delights of his principle residence at Ashridge in Hertfordshire for his more peripheral and altogether less enticing property at Worsley just outside Manchester. Ironically, in yet another twist of fate, if he had been more persistent in his negotiations with Elizabeth all might have been resolved, because Maria died of consumption in 1759, thus removing the obstacle to their marriage.

As it was he was now thoroughly miserable, living in the back of beyond surrounded by little more than an old Hall for a home, no friends and some land, upon which stood a barely functional coal mine. From London dandy he had become, in his favourite racing parlance, an also-ran. At this point he had two choices: to wallow in his grief, perhaps to drink himself into oblivion, or to assume his seigniorial responsibilities as Duke. Luckily for Brindley and the country, he chose the latter.

Being a Duke in mid-eighteenth century England was not something to be sniffed at. By European standards the English aristocracy was a relatively compact coterie and they exercised considerable economic and political power. What was more, as we have seen, they were often quite intimately linked, either through blood or marriage, and would hold lands in several places. The Duke of Newcastle, for example, had land across thirteen different counties. And land it was that often held to key to their fortune. At around this time land values (and therefore rents) rose considerably, as did the price of agricultural produce. Furthermore, the Enclosure Acts were encouraging the more efficient use of land and those rich enough, like the Duke, could invest in new farming technologies to improve yields still further.

These changes were part of the wider shifts taking place in the economic fabric of the country at the time. Although at first sight the Duke's decision to retreat to Manchester could be interpreted as running away to sulk, he was in fact at the crest of a growing wave of interest in the people and resources that existed in the country outside London, the taste of which was becoming rather too rich for some.

Elsewhere in Europe the idea of a Duke taking an interest in trade would have been a complete anathema. By way of contrast, in England many landowners felt that they had almost a responsibility to optimise the benefits of God's bounty. Of course this might mean some investment, but this was at a time when cash was not particularly an issue and the allure of adding yet further to riches can be a powerful motivation, especially if, like Egerton, you have little else to do.

Although London would continue to dominate both economic and political life, its pre-eminence was under threat of challenge from the vast untapped potential of areas such as the North West, North East and the Midlands. In these areas the ingredients for a fundamental shake up in the drivers of the country's wealth sat largely undisturbed. Although largely inaudible, the heavy footsteps of change were approaching.

Having made his decision to make Worsley his home, the Duke understood his need for an agent, and it is at this point that a fourth character should be given due prominence in this chapter. Although not really a patron in the strictest sense of the word, the intervention of John Gilbert, the man the Duke chose to be his agent, turned out to be critical in this story.

Like Wedgwood and the Duke, the course of Gilbert's life was irrevocably altered by the death of his father. In Gilbert's case this took place when he was nineteen and it meant that he had to leave a promising apprenticeship with the firm of Boulton in Birmingham, later to become famous as pioneers of steam when they formed a partnership with James Watt. John was required back home to look after the family's limeworks at Coton. His older brother Thomas, later Earl Gower's agent, had been the one in whom the family had invested an education and he couldn't leave his legal studies in London. When Thomas became free he took over at Coton, but not before completing some legal work for the Duke of Bridgewater at Ashridge and John was introduced to the Duke as a prospective agent, with a particular brief to consider the Duke's mines and how they might be made more profitable.

What happened next forms a later part of this story, suffice to say that this appointment formed the catalyst for bringing together of all the main characters described in this chapter. As a result of this coming together the Duke was to find some purpose for his life, Wedgwood and Gower a way of opening up their beloved Staffordshire to the rest of the world and Gilbert a lifetime's employment and, in time, not inconsiderable wealth.

The link between them all was Brindley, and it is his story we now need to return to.

five

The Duke's Cut

Four miles into the underground streams that take you to the furthest coal seams of Worsley Delph mine you can be forgiven for thinking you have joined the spirits of the dead on the River Lethe of Greek mythology. Alongside the so-called river of forgetfulness, situated deep in the underworld, the dead were said to drink the water so that they could enjoy oblivion and forget the sorrows of their earthly existence prior to entering Elysium.

Encased by rock and far from the familiarity of sunlight and grass, the few miners who volunteered to penetrate the darkness of the Worsley mine must have felt much the same. Inside the labyrinth the silence would only be broken by inhuman noises; the creaking of their craft, distant rumblings from deep within the hillside's soul and the steady drip, drip, drip of water.

Swinging their lanterns on their way to the coal-face they would have seen the long, thin boats under their charge, strung together in groups of five. Made of wood, they had high-ribbed sides on the inside giving them a skeletal appearance, earning them the appropriate nickname of 'starvationers' and adding yet further to the general atmosphere of mortification. Then as now the water would have had an eerie ochreous sheen, a product of the high level of iron hydroxide particles in the ore within the mine, a patina that would have shined like gold in the light of their candles. The channel into the hillside was ten feet wide with just enough headroom to stand and take a swing with a pick.

Ahead of them would be a horse, attached to the front boat by a length of rope and pulling them deeper and deeper into the mine. Once their destination was reached they would stay all day, chipping away at the solid black wall in front of them, filling the boats with coal and sending the horses back unaccompanied to the entrance. There was only one way out, they needed no supervision. Day after day, week after week, year after year the same routine in a fruitless attempt to satisfy the insatiable: the demand for cheap coal in the growing town of Manchester.

The entrance was only six feet wide and when they emerged the daylight would have hit the eyes of man and beast alike with a blow. As they regained their senses and looked around

Nailmakers Cottage, Worsley. This cottage in Worsley housed the only industry in the village before Gilbert and his men got to work, turning out nails.

they would have felt as if they had entered a cavern that had had its roof removed. Sheer-faced granite would have surrounded them on three sides, roughly hewn as if cut in anger.

A huge water bellows constructed out of a hollow tree trunk stood upright and proud behind them on the hillside above the entrance. This ingenious contraption collected water flowing from above the mine entrance and channelled it down into the canal below. In so doing it created a downdraught, which in turn could be used to ventilate the mine shafts themselves, a typically efficient Brindley contraption. In addition, Brindley had set up a permanent fire under the main shaft that created a strong updraught that drew fresh air in from the tunnel's entrance, giving further ventilation.

As the miners stepped off the starvationers, the horses would have been unhitched and their loads transferred into fresh boats to continue their relentless journey over the calm flat surface of the Duke's new waterway towards Manchester. The first landmark they would pass would be the nailmaker's cottage, stranded on an island on its own, about the only building, and certainly the only industry in Worsley, that predated the Duke and his canal. This would be followed swiftly by the ostentatious expanse of the newly-built Packet House, not yet adorned with the half-timbered façade added nearly a century later at the height of the canal's success. Like a bucket chain set up to quell a fire, the routine continued with a mechanical precision and rhythm, although in this case the fire needed stoking not putting out and was a full ten miles away.

What had started out as a notion had become stark reality, transforming the fortunes of the men behind it and the communities at each of its ends. For years the Bridgewaters had dreamed of carrying their coal to Manchester by means other than the untrustworthy and inefficient roads. Even the turnpikes were insufficient for the task, given the bulk of material involved. Water was the obvious answer, a horse can pull sixty times more weight if it is carried on water rather than its back, but water was only available part of the way.

This potential was well understood. Navigable rivers were already part of the country's transport infrastructure and occasionally there were attempts to improve them. As long ago as 1720 an Act of Parliament had established the Mersey & Irwell Navigation Company to take tolls and maintain the two rivers in its name, carrying boats into the heart of Manchester. Elsewhere rivers such as the Thames, the Aire and Calder, and the Don provided valuable employment to rivermen and kept the wheels of commerce oiled. The problem was that rivers went only where nature intended, which was not necessarily the same as where man wanted to go.

As such, only rarely could they provide a complete route for cargo, requiring goods to be lifted on and off boats to the inconvenience of all concerned. Rivers silted, flooded and went dry on you. What was more, they were not the most efficient mode of transport, with boats usually pulled by men rather than horses, and where a river was tidal there were usually only certain times of the day when forward passage was possible.

In 1737 the first Duke of Bridgewater had gone to Parliament to gain permission to convert the Worsley Brook that ran into and out of his mines into an artificial river. In effect this gave him permission to buy the land he didn't already own in order to execute what was little more than an idea, no formal feasibility study of the economics or logistics of the scheme being required.

In the end nothing came of the plan, it being beaten down through a combination of affordability (it was far too expensive) and opposition from vested interests, notably the turnpikes and the Mersey & Irwell Navigation Company, despite the fact that the plan was to link the mine to the Irwell. Although in theory this would have added to the company's revenues, they were concerned about the possible effect on their water supply, a constant worry for river companies and rivermen alike.

Instead, in the great British tradition, things were allowed to muddle along. Although growing towns, both Manchester and Liverpool were still too small at this time to demand attention. Their inherent potential was just that, untapped and to a large extent not really understood. This was still an agrarian economy where there was a poor appreciation of the impact of organised labour. In 1724 Manchester contained only 2,400 families. Thirty years later the combined population of Manchester and Salford was 20,000, mostly engaged in manufacture of one sort or another.

As with the potters of Staffordshire, these craftsmen were working mainly for themselves and by themselves, although their families and the occasional apprentice might also be involved. Whilst the potters of Stoke had their wheels and fire, the Mancunians had spinning wheels and handlooms. Their products were a combination of crude fabrics, not dissimilar to corduroy, made from wool, and small specialist items such as leather laces for women's bodices or shoe-ties.

As the town grew so it became more complex, with the more successful of the manufacturers reaching out into the town's hinterland both to sell their wares and to gather in raw materials. Their Ford Transit vans were their pack horses, their motorways the mill roads, so called because they were traditionally used by donkeys taking oats to a mill, and turnpikes. Takings were at risk from highwaymen and supplies in and out of the town were erratic at best. It wasn't until 1758 that the first private coach was kept in Manchester, up until then there had simply been no point in having one.

For most the only formal transport was the coach to London that left three times a week from the Royal Oak Inn. Called the London and Manchester Machine, the coach was advertised regularly in the *Manchester Mercury* with copy that stated that it would 'set out every Tuesday, Thursday and Saturday morning at 5 o'clock [in the morning] and would be in London every Tuesday, Thursday and Saturday night'. Each passage cost the substantial sum of £2 5s and for that passengers were allowed fourteen pounds weight of luggage only – each extra pound being charged at threepence. Outside passengers and children that travelled 'on lap' were half price. The advertisements were careful to state that no money, plate, watches, writings etc. would be answerable for unless entered and paid for accordingly. Finally, the owners of the coach were careful to stress that the service would be provided 'God willing'.

The roads were so bad at this time that food supplies could not be guaranteed. When the roads were waterlogged, Manchester effectively became a town under siege, getting by on what it had hoarded or could raise, although little of any nutritional value was grown on the poor earth surrounding the town.

Food riots were common. One such had taken place in November 1757, which led to a subsequent rebuttal in the *Manchester Mercury* from Messrs Brammel and Hatfield whose Travis Mill had been completely destroyed. As if the loss of their grain had not been enough they also stood to lose their reputation. It was common at the time to blame the cornbrokers for shortages and the rumour had been spread that they had been adulterating their flour. In their plea they stated that reports that they had 'great quantities of acorn, dried white beans, horse dung, chopped straw, peas and bones' already in their hoppers ready to be 'ground down with corn and made into flour for the use and consumption of the public' were completely untrue.

It wasn't a shortage of food that worried the Duke of Bridgewater however. The same constraints that prevented food getting into the town also prevented a steady supply of the mainstay fuel: coal. The irony was that Manchester was surrounded by coal; it was just very hard to transport it. Like everything else it had to go by horse or mule. The standard weight was 280 pounds, as much as could be carried in two baskets each thirty inches by twenty and ten inches deep. Although coal might be sold for ten pence the horseload at the pithead, its price would double in the few miles between there and the town.

Although the Duke's mine was actually quite close to the Irwell, which could take his output into the heart of Manchester, the act of loading and unloading made it barely worthwhile; that and the three shillings and fourpence a ton toll the Navigation Company charged, however far a load was travelling. Furthermore, the Navigation Company was making it easier for his competitors to undercut the market for his coal in Liverpool.

Despite this the demand for coal from Manchester was rising all the time. As we have seen, the age of the steam engine was yet to come and manufacturing was still small scale, but the growing population needed to keep warm and cook, and in a town there was no forest to forage wood from.

Some kind of waterway it had to be.

* * * * * * * * * *

The decaying workings outside Worsley's mine entrance before they were cleaned up. (Courtesy of Manchester Central Library)

The idea of an artificial 'cut' was not a new one. Francis Egerton would have seen the canals of France and Italy on his Grand Tour, notably the Canal du Midi, which had been open for eighty years, and Brindley himself had already been employed on surveying part of a possible canal to connect the Trent and the Mersey.

An English canal had even been cut in 1757 by the Corporation of Liverpool, alongside the Sankey Brook and linking the Mersey about two miles below Warrington to St Helens, Gerrard Bridge and Penny Bridge. The first half of the eighteenth century had seen the number of navigable river miles grow by about a quarter, but this had been a slow process and one nearing its natural limits.

Not even Brindley's most ardent advocate could claim that he invented canals. What he did proceed to do following his association with the Duke of Bridgewater and John Gilbert was perfect the technology that made them viable. Canals gave him an arena to display and develop his undoubted strengths, including the ability to understand and appreciate local topography, as exercised in the design of wind and watermills, his well-demonstrated affinity with water and his various skills as stonemason, bricklayer, blacksmith and carpenter.

The idea of building an artificial waterway from Worsley was almost certainly John Gilbert's. It was he who had gone some way to solving the Duke's other main headache: the constant need to drain flood water from his mine. Mining techniques were at the time still relatively crude, as was the technology used to drain them. This consisted mainly of men lowering and pulling up buckets of water, which proved to be totally inadequate at Worsley, or the driving of a shaft into the mine to drain water out from it to a lower level, as Brindley had done at the Wet Earth Colliery. This had been done at Worsley, but not very well, adding to the cost of maintaining the mine.

A canal would kill three birds with one stone: a means of draining the mine, a independent supply of water for the canal and a way of getting the coal to market. Indeed, not even Gilbert can claim exclusivity on the idea of a canal. As we have seen, the Duke's father had had the idea but it had fallen at the twin hurdles of practicality and cost. Working with the Duke, Gilbert was, however, the first to try to realise the dream.

On being appointed the Duke's agent in 1757 Gilbert examined the mines at Worsley and weighed up the complexities of both extracting the coal and transporting it to market. In an act that showed that Brindley didn't hold the monopoly on solitary thinking, Gilbert duly retired to his bed at the Bull Hotel in Manchester and refused to see anyone for two days while he mulled the problem over.

Eventually happy with his solution, he settled up with the innkeeper and rode over to Worsley where he explained his plans to the Duke. His big idea was to take boats right up to where the coal was mined, thus obviating the need to wind it up shafts. This would necessitate the cutting of a series of waterways into the solid rock that led down to the coal but would be worth it because it would provide a means of draining the mine at the same time: an elegant and neat solution. Being a man of imagination, as well as someone who had seen canals work abroad, the Duke grasped the concept immediately and with the energy of the young went about putting the plan into action.

Work had therefore been underway for some time before Brindley became involved. However, get involved he did. As work progressed it must have become increasingly clear to Gilbert that he needed some support. However ingenious he was he couldn't solve everything and his expertise lay more in the mines than in the channelling and control of water.

This contemporary line drawing of the original Barton Aqueduct shows how sailing craft designed for use on rivers were used initially on the new canal before purpose-built craft were created. (Courtesy of Manchester Central Library)

It is highly likely that both the Duke and Gilbert would have known of Brindley independently, not simply by reputation but possibly in person too, certainly in the case of the latter. His work at the Wet Earth Colliery couldn't have failed to have reached the Duke's ears, as it took place only a few miles from Worsley. Furthermore, Brindley's involvement in surveying a section of the proposed Trent to Mersey canal would have been carried out under the auspices of John Gilbert's brother Thomas, the Earl of Gower's agent. Finally, Brindley had also worked for Samuel Egerton, who had been the Duke's guardian when he was younger. It truly was a small world.

What they would have heard they would probably have liked. Brindley's inventiveness, experience and general sense of daring would have been exactly the cocktail they would have empathised with, perhaps seeing a little of themselves in this man. When they finally met, Brindley's generally dour demeanour must have been taken as part of the package as he was given full reign to conduct what he later called an 'ocular survey' on horseback.

Brindley was first called to Worsley Hall on 1 July 1759, staying on this occasion for a total of six days. According to his journal he was to spend a total of 51 days at the Duke's home through the remainder of the year, balancing his time there with his continuing work with steam and 'about the navigation'. The waterway he was referring to in his diary however, was not the Duke's but Earl Gower's proposed project. This work trailed him around much of northern Staffordshire, with mentions made in his journals of visits in May to Lichfield, Newcastle under Lyme and Tamworth, although it wasn't until April 1762 that Brindley was finally able to record payment 'for the Staffordshire'.

Worsley Hall was a magnificent half-timbered house standing in its own wooded grounds and would become well known to Brindley. Rectangular in shape with two small wings and a courtyard in between, it would become his second home over the subsequent months, the site of many long discussions late into the night between himself, the Duke and Gilbert – a group Josiah Wedgwood later labelled 'The Triumvirate'.

The original idea had been to take the canal from the mine to Salford, outside Manchester, and this was the route set out in the original Act of Parliament obtained by the Duke. About the time of Brindley's involvement this plan was modified drastically to stretch the canal to Stretford, better known today through its connections with Manchester United's football ground. This would take the coal much closer to its market in the heart of Manchester and also allow it to link up with the proposed Trent & Mersey Canal, details of which Brindley would have been aware following his preliminary surveying work the year before.

This was big thinking for it meant somehow taking the canal over the River Irwell. Although the advantage of cutting out the men from the Navigation was an attractive one, it wasn't without its difficulties. At first the thinking was to build two flights of locks, one either side of the valley, with boats from the mine crossing the river. This promised to be a massive enterprise that would not only be costly but also keep the whole project in thrall to the whims of the Navigation Company, who would remain free to charge even for this short passage. What was more it would add considerably to the time needed to complete the canal and the Duke was a man in a hurry to start realising some income from his investment.

It was then that an alternative, even more radical solution was proposed. Rather than cross the river on its surface, why not go over it altogether? Why not build an aqueduct at Barton, five miles west of Manchester? The simple answer of course would have been because no one had ever done it before in England and both the technology and skills required were unproven, but this was brushed aside.

Some have challenged whether this was indeed Brindley's idea, pointing out that the Duke himself was no mean engineer and would have seen aqueducts during his Grand Tour of Europe. Notably he would have seen the one on the Martesan Canal near Milan over the River Molgora, which although not as daring as that proposed at Barton still had three spans of thirty feet each. What we do know is that Brindley suddenly became occupied in a reconnaissance of the proposition and without even retiring to bed returned with a swift response that, yes, the idea was possible. The project was on.

The history of the Bridgewater Canal, and indeed much of Brindley's story, is littered with disputes over who had which idea and when. Such arguments are largely redundant however, as proof for different claims is rarely available. The reality is that the story of the Duke's canal is the story of three men, each of whom made a different contribution and all of whom shared ideas together well into the night over a bottle or three from the Duke's cellar. Anyone who has spent nights putting the world to rights over a drink can testify that in the morning the ownership of a good idea is usually less important than its worth.

Wherever the idea of the aqueduct originated it was a daring and inspirational one. Not only did it offer the prospect of solving the problem of how best to reach the market for the Duke's coal, but it cut the Navigation Company out of the equation and involved a spectacular edifice that was bound to capture the imagination and cement the canal's future. Although success would deliver a spectacular propaganda coup, this was far from guaranteed. Not only did the aqueduct represent a major engineering challenge, but in order to be constructed embankments would be required on either side to reach the flat level of the canal. More importantly, on a practical level these new plans exceeded the powers the Duke had been granted by Parliament. He would need a fresh Act of Parliament.

Two years of hell stood in front of Wedgwood's 'triumvirate' before they would begin to be taken seriously, years that would see all three driven to physical exhaustion and almost make the Duke bankrupt. At first the general consensus was that the Duke had surely gone mad, this canal project of his was probably some kind of folly. Memories of the family dunce and the society playboy who made a fool of himself over an Irish floozy would have lingered.

From the middle of 1759 onwards the three men were frequently cloistered together at the Old Hall mulling over the best way forward, with Brindley even living at the Hall for long periods, his continuing bachelor status no doubt making this a convenient arrangement. During the day Brindley would set to work on a preliminary survey of the canal and Gilbert on the mines. At night they would each share problems and ideas they had encountered. Sometimes these discussions would wander, taking in issues of philosophy and religion, and during the rest of his life one of Brindley's most treasured possessions was a prayer book given to him by the Duke at this time, that he later had bound.

There is a suspicion that the Duke, who was also a bachelor at this time, prompted many of these late night discussions. By this time he had committed everything to the project and had some right to feel anxious about its success. During this period, and for a number of years to come, he was a restless soul, perhaps, in modern parlance, he was trying to 'find himself' or at least a purpose to his otherwise empty life. If there was ever a lull in the conversation, and

The size of Brindley's home at Turnhust, seen here just before its demolition, gives a good idea of how successful he was in his own lifetime. (Courtesy of The Waterways Archive)

perhaps a suggestion of bed from the older Brindley, the Duke would leap up and bang his barometer, treating his captive audience to an amateur weather forecast for the next day.

After forty-six days of this Brindley had prepared his plans so as to maximise their chances of success before Parliament, and in the late winter of 1759 Bridgewater petitioned Parliament for an Act to cut a canal east from his mines to Salford on the outskirts of Manchester and west to link up with the Mersey. Early in 1760 the Duke took the tedious coach to London to shepherd his second Act through Parliament. Meanwhile, Gilbert and Brindley supervised those works they already had permission for, whilst completing a detailed survey of the proposed new route. This survey was completed in January 1760, at which point Brindley joined the Duke in London, preferring to travel on horseback rather than brave the coach, a journey that took him five days.

An alternative plan to build an artificial waterway into Manchester from the coalfields of Wigan had been defeated by the same old vested interests in 1753 and the new Act was certainly no 'shoo-in'. Mindful of these objectors the Duke was ready with concessions and some promises. The most important of these was a commitment not to sell coal at more than four pence a hundredweight – less than half the average price – and to hold to this promise for forty years, a rash and almost ridiculous guarantee, but a mark of his determination to win the day.

Another concession was to allow certain cargoes, such as manure and lime, to be carried free. In line with the general attitude towards property though, the Duke was able to insert a passage that stipulated that all toll dodgers were to be levied with a forty-shilling fine. Perhaps not surprisingly the Duke's Second Act passed without opposition. Either the

Duke was going to deliver the impossible or he was mad. Either way, it was going to be entertaining to watch.

While all this had been going on Gilbert had been busy with the mine, doing work that didn't require fresh permission. Even at the most basic level of the project, however, the Duke encountered problems. The plan to drive through the rockface at Worsley and into the mine was fundamental to the whole idea, but progress was slow. Mining tools at that time had barely advanced since the Iron Age, being picks with steel tips that needed constant sharpening. It was disheartening work, chipping away at solid rock with sparks as the main output of your efforts.

At one point the men involved decided to strike or, less dramatically, to bypass Gilbert and appeal direct to the Duke as to the pointlessness of their cause. After hearing their petition, the Duke took a snuffbox, a relic perhaps from his more carefree days, and took a pinch of snuff out. 'Can you get that much powder out from the rock between you all?' he asked. The men conceded that they could, at which point the Duke instructed them that 'As long as you can get a pinch out you should continue to work and I shall continue to pay you.' Suitably chastened, the men returned to work, a reminder ringing in their ears that their future work as miners depended upon a successful breaching of the rock.

Fortified by this vote of confidence from his master, Gilbert pressed home his advantage and even began to commission the building of boats to take the coal to Manchester once it had been extracted. To his credit though, he did later discover the virtues of using dynamite to blast his way through to the seam. The Duke was also taking the long view, and there is evidence that from the very beginning of the enterprise he was setting aside sums to pay those who became sick or injured in its execution.

Although Brindley was busy on the Duke's behalf during this phase of the work he had not given up on his other work. Canals were still a somewhat speculative enterprise and he had only recently had his pride scorched through his involvement with steam engines – although as we will see this was an obsession which still had some mileage in it.

What seems more likely is that the embers of his interest in this new field, kindled on his work on the proposed Trent to Mersey Canal, were being fanned during this time with the Duke and Gilbert. Whilst working on that survey he had displayed his customary eye for detail, suggesting where it would be necessary to site bridges, fords and fences and measuring the fall of the water, suggesting that it had been more than simply another job. It would have been impossible not to be moved by the ambition and enthusiasm of his two new colleagues and, as we know, once he was convinced something was possible Brindley was as tenacious as a bulldog.

It is also possible that in canals he had found the fresh challenge he had been seeking when he had found himself drawn to the power of steam. Water, and how to control it, was his specialist subject. Engineering solutions out of problems was his forte. The further he went with this project, it seems reasonable to assume, the more stimulation he got out of it.

There was another possible attraction – the Duke's money. Although Brindley was careful with money, he could never be accused of being ruthless in his pursuit of a fortune. Indeed, his pocket books show that during this time he went back to charging quite modest daily rates for his contribution. Working for the Duke gave the promise of some kind of security of income – the man was a Duke after all – and of challenge at someone else's risk, which was more than could be said for his dabbling in steam.

During this time Brindley raised the grand sum of £5,431 6s 8d to buy a quarter share of the Turnhurst Estate, near Stafford, which was eventually to become his home. His fellow purchasers were Thomas Gilbert, John's brother, his own brother John and a certain Mr Henshall, who shall feature again later in this story. It is likely that this purchase drained his immediate cash reserves, whilst at the same time placing him in the debt of a neighbour in Leek, giving a further reason for avoiding speculative work on his own account. Little was he to know that the canal, now becoming known as 'The Duke's Cut' was to precipitate the most uncertain period of his entire career so far.

★ ★ ★ ★ ★ ★ ★ ★ ★ ★

With the second Act passed the triumvirate decided to concentrate wholly on a route into Manchester, avoiding the Irwell altogether and putting on ice the idea of pushing out towards Liverpool as well, despite the fact that the Duke had already paid out over £4,000 for the land where he had intended to build his docks there. This decision had in part been forced upon them by continued opposition from the Navigation Company, which refused to agree a reasonable rate for junctions to be cut into the river.

At the same time the opportunity was taken to incorporate a few branches from the proposed canal and to take it right up to the mouth of the mine at Worsley. Given his experience with water, Brindley was a natural for the task of draining the mines and channelling the water to places where it could be most useful for the overall scheme. Whilst waiting for the second Act to pass, further work had taken place and patches of canal could be found along the route like unconnected pieces of jigsaw.

To the neutral observer this enterprise of the Duke's must have seemed ambitious in the extreme. A completely artificial waterway cut over this distance required a new and untested technology. It wasn't immediately obvious, for example, why the water wouldn't simply seep out of the ditches cut into the land. Also, if it wasn't flowing wouldn't it go stagnant? How would the boats move? How could anyone be sure that the massive new embankment outside Barton was stable? In days when only the few read newspapers, if indeed they could read at all, there was only word of mouth to answer these questions, and that required some kind of common understanding amongst those likely to be asked – the workmen – which was unlikely to be forthcoming.

As the scheme progressed and grew, it is hardly surprising that the Duke was seen by more and more people to be throwing his family's fortune away. They were not alone in this fear. As the project went on it became clear to the Duke, Gilbert and Brindley that their original cost estimates, probably never anything more than a rough sketch and certainly not a sophisticated business plan, were wildly out. The tradition of massive cost over-runs on large capital engineering projects was born.

Like most such projects at this time, the canal was entirely privately financed. The South Sea Bubble in 1720 had resulted in laws that restricted the formation of private companies and the raising of finance through shares. Forming a private company still required a Royal Charter. In time the Duke spent £220,000 of his own money to get the whole canal built

– an absolute fortune, the equivalent to an individual financing an entire motorway out of his own pocket in modern times.

Perhaps it was a mixture of pride and bloody-mindedness, a determination to prove that he was right, that drove him on. He was also a young man, only twenty-three, and no doubt eager to make his mark. Something in his gut must have told him he was right. These were economically optimistic times and the upbeat mood must have permeated the venture. The population had been rising since the early 1730s, bringing with it increased economic activity and demand as well as a pool of cheap labour, as the growth of Manchester all too vividly demonstrated. What's more, less people were dying prematurely, as food got better and sanitation improved. The time was right for something like canals.

As the costs of the canal began to hurt, the Duke began to cut back on his personal living expenses, reducing them at one point to a mere £400 a year. This required him to reduce his staff right down to a groom and a manservant and to move into the Hall's gatehouse. All three of the triumvirate could be found lending their shoulders to the wheel. On one occasion Brindley, whose Quaker background encouraged him to dress plainly, was taken for a 'mere peasant, no better than one of his carters', and the Duke in turn was at one point taken for one of his own labourers when he was asked to help lever a sack of coal onto the back of a customer in his coalyard, something he did without complaint.

Brindley's thoughts at this time seem to have been confined to the mental challenge the canal represented. Despite, or perhaps because of, his recent investment in property he was less exposed to failure on a financial level than the Duke, who until the canal was completed faced the constant prospect of ruin. Gilbert also stood to lose his job if the Duke went under and might find getting another difficult if he was seen as the man who had egged the young Duke on through his madness.

Brindley on the other hand had a cartload of skills he could fall back on. His enterprise and fortitude would see him all right, even if it might take some time to get over a potential failure. Not that this option ever seemed to enter his mind. Rather, it was the constant supply of fresh mental challenges offered by the canal, and in particular the aqueduct at Barton, that seemed to drive him on.

A good example of this was the various streams that ran across the proposed route of the canal that would need to be controlled through weirs. Although this approach had served him well in the past it was one of Brindley's fundamental principles of canal building that the waters from different sources should never be allowed to mix other than when needed for supply. This was because of the dangers of introducing tidal water or unpredictable surges into the canal, which was to be, as far as possible, a totally self-contained entity.

One particular example of this was where the canal reached its end in Manchester and joined the River Medlock. To avoid the river intermingling with his canal Brindley created a weir in the shape of six segments of a circle with a circumference of 366 yards, each segment built of squared stone and bound together with iron, over which the water flowed into a lower level and from there into a well before flowing into the Irwell itself via an underground passage. In a typical Brindleyesque touch he had also added a water-wheel, which was powered by the excess water, which in turn powered two hoists, one to lift the coal as it arrived at its destination, the other being located in the warehouse of certain Messrs Gilbert and Henshall.

Meanwhile work on the canal continued. Although they were in a hurry, both Gilbert and Brindley continued the tradition they had started of efficient solutions to practical problems. In the same way that the water from the mines irrigated the canal, rock from the mine was brought down the open sections of the canal and used to build the aqueduct, sandstone from the mine was used to construct bridges over the canal and rubble from the quarrying was used to reinforce the embankments.

Along the way there were of course the inevitable hitches. At one point the canal burst its banks causing widespread flooding and destruction. Although this was thankfully on the Duke's land the damage would have been to tenants' crops and they wouldn't have been impressed. Although the culprit was probably moles rather than any design fault with the canal, something had to be done. This was exactly the sort of challenge Brindley relished and he designed a solution involving wooden gates that sat on the bottom of the canal with heavy weights on them. The idea was that if the banks broke, the weights would move and the platforms would rise to form a temporary dam.

As a solution this was reasonably successful but not foolproof, but this is to miss the point. By acting quickly the Duke was able to demonstrate his sensitivity to the concerns of others, even those who owed him some fealty, and, just as importantly, prove once again an aptitude for good public relations when executing a contentious project that some modern civil engineers could possibly learn from.

With the project firing on all cylinders things stepped up a gear in the autumn of 1760. At Barton the foundations for the piers of the bridge had been dug, going down fifty feet. Gilbert was literally buying time, tipping boatmen on the river to pass through quickly when he

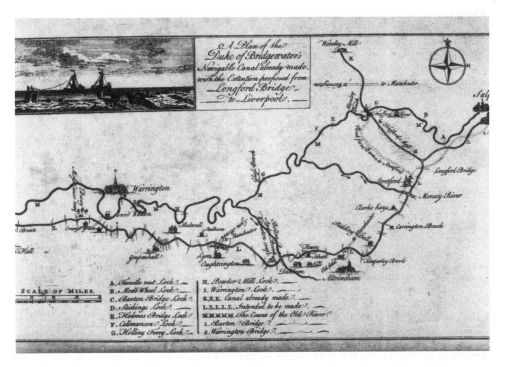

Plan of the Duke of Bridgewater's Navigable Canal. (Courtesy of Manchester Central Library)

needed to drain a pound and paying his own men 'rain money' to carry on working through the torrential downpours that part of the world can get in the autumn months.

It was in digging the foundations for the bridge that Gilbert made another discovery that was to provide a further contribution to the self-sufficiency of the project. In digging down he came across a seam of lime marl and he decided to conduct a few experiments with it. After a few failures he discovered that if it was ground down to a powder and mixed with coal dust it could be burnt in a kiln and then mixed with sand to produce a waterproof mortar. This discovery was to prove invaluable in the construction of bridges that had to stand partly in water and saved having to source lime from thirty miles away. Over the course of the canal this single discovery is estimated to have saved the Duke £2,000.

As the piers were sunk and the aqueduct began to take on its final shape it is understandable that attention turned to Barton. It became clear that the Duke would complete his folly, the question had now become would it work? To most rational people the very idea defied logic, to carry that weight of water over a bridge in the sky, and then to float boats over the heads of other boats in the river below was surely crazy? Friends lobbied the Duke for a second opinion and eventually he caved in, whether to silence his critics, to buy time or for his own peace of mind we do not know. Whichever, it must have come as a shock when the engineer, almost certainly the pioneer civil engineer John Smeaton, came out against the scheme, declaring it impractical.

To his eternal credit the Duke, perhaps in too deep by now, stuck by Brindley, satisfied by his plain speaking common sense that the Duke found hard to fault. By now the aqueduct had become a *cause célèbre*, and people began to visit simply to see its tall stone arches being erected and no doubt to share opinions on where the project was weakest.

As if the aqueduct wasn't enough, the embankments on either side of the structure that needed to be constructed to raise the level of the canal were a marvel of engineering in their own right. One even incorporated a tunnel to take the main Warrington to Manchester road. This too seemed like the act of madmen, as surely common sense dictated that the water in the canal would soak through the soft earth of the embankment, saturate it and cause it to slip?

So it was that the Duke and his trusted advisers, as well as invited guests, found themselves in the midst of the summer of 1761 watching in awe as the first boat laden with coal approached the new bridge.

What followed is history.

six

Chalk and Cheese

The one thing that Brindley and his colleagues could never have anticipated now happened – the aqueduct became a tourist attraction. Word spread fast, in the inns, on the turnpike and in the fledgling newspapers of the day. To those that had heard of it the idea of a river suspended in mid air defied credence and quite literally had to be seen to be believed.

When they came some were happy to stop and stare. The massive bridge was a modern marvel, dazzling in its sheer scale. Completed in only a year, it was surely the work of a genius. Others were mystified by the seemingly miraculous act of a single horse pulling great loads of coal apparently without effort, plodding along gently without complaint or need for rest, and had to get closer to see how it was done. Particularly striking to those used to the barely controlled chaos of the turnpike would have been the relative silence and serenity of the scene. It was actually possible to hear the water lap the sides of the canal as a boat went by.

The bravest of all, however, would climb the embankment and approach the towpath before gingerly stepping out along the 'water-bridge' itself. For these few the aqueduct had become the white-knuckle ride of its day, crossing it an act of bravado young men would put each other up to. Like tightrope walkers they would put one foot on the battlement of the bridge and advance slowly, looking forward and proceeding with confidence, going beyond the point of no return before they dared to sneak a look down.

Forty feet below them boats would ply the Irwell in silence, some with sails set into the wind, others pulled by a team of a dozen men oblivious to the fact they were being spied upon. The effect must have been surreal in an age before even hot air balloons, giving those that dared to cross a God-like feeling, not to say an adrenaline rush.

On seeing the aqueduct for the first time one lady visitor reported that it was *'perhaps the greatest artificial curiosity in the world'*, although we do not know what her experience of the world would have been. This unexpected interest was a feature of the canal that the Duke seemed happy to exploit. Having been derided as a fool it must have been hugely satisfying for him to respond to requests from the great and good of the day to see his new marvel.

Brindley's aqueduct became a victim of its own success, with its narrow gauge leading to constant bottlenecks, as illustrated by this early photograph showing coal carriers queuing to cross over the river. (Courtesy of The Waterways Archive)

Men and women alike would write to the Duke and before long he had instituted a booking system, with tickets permitting not only a trip along the canal, but penetration of the mine itself. In setting out what she would get for her money the Duke described in a letter to 'a Lady' how the party would enter the narrow portal to the mine on a starvationer with only lighted candles for illumination and sink a full thousand yards into the heart of the mine, pulling themselves along by means of a rail. Trippers were promised the prospect of watching colliers at work – something the working men must have relished – and if it was all too much glasses of wine would be made available to revive those faint of heart.

One such visitor was Josiah Wedgwood, who became captivated by the canal. A frequent guest at Earl Gower's home at Trentham, records show how he would linger at Worsley, riding along the canal in a boat or beside it on horseback, towards Manchester and back. Even four years after the opening of the aqueduct Wedgwood was writing to Dr Erasmus Darwin describing a trip in which he had been drawn by mule at a leisurely pace for an hour and a half along the canal, and how much he had enjoyed the scenery.

Even later, in 1768, the commentator Arthur Young wrote: *'the effect of coming to Barton Bridge and looking down upon a large river, with barges of great burden towing along it, and up another river, hung in the air, with barges sailing upon it, form altogether a scenery somewhat like enchantment'*, adding that *'the number of foreigners who have visited the Duke of Bridgewater's present navigation is surprising'*. The following year the Duke took advantage of this interest by opening a Packet Boat passenger service along the length of the canal, something that proved to be both popular and lucrative until it was eventually usurped by the railway. The Packet Boat became the

Duke's pride and joy and he ruled that it should have precedence over all other traffic on his water. A postillion armed with a bugle made sure that his will was enforced.

Although all this must have been terrific fun, the canal had a serious purpose and work continued to drive it onwards towards its goal in Manchester. The spectacle and ceremony of the aqueduct's opening was critical in proving to the Duke's detractors and backers that he was on to something, but it also had another effect. In one short moment the future had been revealed and the race was on to be part of it. All those others who had been considering the possibilities of canals, but had lacked either the resolve or the funds to do anything about it, had had a wake up call.

Barton had acted like a rod poked into a wasps' nest. Suddenly everyone wanted a piece of the action, and although the Duke was king of the heap at that moment he had enough insight to see how his bravery in backing Brindley's plans could evaporate if he didn't press home his advantage rapidly. Despite being exhausted, and still in serious financial difficulties, he had no option but to press ahead with phase two of his grand plan. It wouldn't take much for those who had paid Brindley to survey a section of the proposed Trent to Mersey canal only two years before to regroup and constitute a significant threat to the Duke's vision of supplying Liverpool as well as Manchester. There was nothing for it but to revive plans to extend the cut south and west across northern Cheshire towards the Mersey.

Not only would this mean working on two fronts but it would also mean returning to London yet again for a fresh Act of Parliament, the planning permission of its day. Within six weeks of their triumph at Barton the Duke had Brindley out with his surveying gang drawing up a route to Runcorn at the point of the Mersey estuary, which would take boats the final fifteen miles to Liverpool.

During this time Brindley not only had to satisfy the Duke's urgent need for a survey but he had to catch up on other outstanding bits of work neglected in the rush to meet the Barton deadline. His journals record one week in Autumn beginning with 'Set out at dawn to level for Liverpool, levelling and reconnoitring', followed the next week by 'Finish the upper level to Hempstones', which is where it was planned to end the canal. At that point the Duke and Earl Gower set off for London, so Brindley seized the chance to catch up on some other work while they awere away, spending two days at the Congleton silk mill, three days at Trentham for the Earl and a further three days for Earl Stamford before returning to Worsley.

He doesn't seem to have taken any kind of holiday during this period with the single exception recorded in his journals of taking a day off for the 'crounation of Georg [King George III] and Sharlot [Charlotte]'. At this point he took stock, making a note to himself that 'The number of days at Worsley before going to London – 133'. The Duke was running up a considerable bill. After visiting London himself with the Duke both Christmas Day and New Year's Eve were spent at Worsley Hall.

It is hardly surprising, given this heavy workload, that his journals also record him working on the Sabbath, although he restricted himself on these days to 'reconnoitring' rather than full scale surveying. It is likely that Brindley found himself working every hour God sent, even on Sundays, the day his Lord had set aside for His honour, fired in part by the challenges being put before him and partly by the opportunities he could no doubt see emerging. Despite the scope of these opportunities Brindley continued to keep his fingers in a number of pies during this time. Canals, however exciting, were still not sufficiently robust a proposition to stake his future career on.

In fact this time marks the beginning of a level of activity that barely abated for more than a decade. Remember that this was a man already into his forties, and however sound his constitution and fitness levels, honed by a life spent outdoors, this was to be a punishing schedule. By November the survey was complete.

Then as now there was little love lost between the towns of Manchester and Liverpool. However, once they had fully understood the benefits they each stood to gain from the proposed Duke's Cut pragmatism kicked in. The two towns were in fact mutually interdependent, with Liverpool being Manchester's natural port, the place from which its manufactured goods could reach their wider markets and from which it sourced its supplies.

Communications between the two towns had before that point relied on the unpredictability of the Mersey and Irwell Navigation, with its tides, floods and silt; or ordinary roads, with their ruts, tolls and mud. One contemporary described the Navigation as 'tedious, expensive and liable to great interruption', whilst it wasn't until later that the roads were good enough to allow a coach service to develop, and even then it took six or eight horses to pull it through the ditches. Those hardy enough to undertake the journey would have been wise to pass on the breakfast offered at the Prescott stop given the ordeal before them and rely instead on the coach making its estimated arrival at supper time.

Even by the time the Barton Aqueduct opened, an estimated 2,000 tons of goods were being carried each year on the thirty miles of roads between the two towns, with the volume rising all the time. Not only were supplies random but they were expensive, with carriage costing up to two pounds a ton. The river however, was little better, with carriage here costing around twelve shillings a ton, although cargoes were subject to frustrating delays, sometimes getting stuck for days or weeks waiting for the right tide.

Like Manchester, Liverpool was a relatively new town and suffered from all the usual deficiencies of this condition. It had only really taken off in the early part of the century when the silting up of the River Dee had cut the traditional port of Chester off from the sea. A series of new docks built after 1709 allowed Liverpool to grow quickly and the symbiotic relationship with Manchester to develop.

By the middle of the eighteenth century Liverpool was a microcosm of many similar towns in England. Vibrant and busy, these two cauldrons of activity were outgrowing their immediate hinterland and needed to forge links with other up-and-coming centres to realise their potential. The country was a scattered jigsaw, waiting for someone or something to put the pieces together to make a whole picture.

* * * * * * * * * *

If the stretch from Worsley to Manchester can be looked at as the gaping jaws of a snake, the line to Runcorn was its tail – twice as long and almost as challenging in engineering terms. The Duke had little option but to press on, despite the fact that the economics of the still to be completed Manchester line had yet to be proven. If he needed proof of his concerns that he was in danger of losing his early-mover advantage the Duke had to look no further than Brindley.

This photograph of Worsley in winter conjures up an evocative and unlikely image of a village that can reasonably claim to be the first industrial centre in Britain. (Courtesy of The Waterways Archive)

No employee, Brindley was free to take commissions from whomever he chose and within weeks requests were coming in to survey other canals, including the proposed Trent to Mersey canal, as the Duke had no doubt predicted, as well as a Chester Canal, a proposed navigation up the River Dee to Bangor and on to Shrewsbury, and another proposed navigation between Rotherham and Doncaster.

No doubt increasingly conscious of the possibility of losing his prime asset, the Duke finally settled his outstanding account with Brindley in July 1762. This covered 302 days work dating back to Christmas 1760, the modern equivalent of working full time, although as we have seen Brindley's full time was vastly different from ours, excluding as it does weekends and holidays, if not high-days. The sum involved was a little over 100 pounds, suggesting an average rate of pay of seven shillings a day, although Brindley did enjoy free board and lodging for himself and his trusty horse at Worsley whilst working for the Duke. A separate record in the Duke's accounts valued this at a further twelve shillings a week.

This payment would have followed the successful passing of yet another Act of Parliament, required to gain permission to stretch the canal to Liverpool, and would have been a recognition both of the Duke's confidence of future riches and of Brindley's role in helping him to secure the permission he so critically needed.

Prior to taking the journey to London, success was something neither of them could have taken for granted. The Duke's transparent energy and ambition had begun to make him enemies. He was also challenging the existing economic establishment, both those who saw turnpikes as the future and more specifically the owners of the Mersey and Irwell Navigation. However flawed, this was a useful source of income for its backers. Whilst they might be able to stand some competition on part of the route into Manchester, an alternative into Liverpool, and what was more, one that would be both reliable and cheaper, represented a real threat to the Navigation's viability.

Their initial response, if anything, had the effect of galvanising the Duke's resolve. They offered to reduce the rate per ton for coal to a mere sixpence a ton on the stretch between Barton and Manchester if the Duke agreed to terminate his new canal at the aqueduct. When this failed they offered him some exclusive benefits for using their waterway. The Duke resisted, convinced he had his main competitor on the run.

The Duke and his men had already been in the capital in the late summer and autumn of 1761, the triumphs of Barton still fresh in their minds. On this trip they had laid the foundations for getting their new Act, but on their return it would have become immediately clear that this was not be to like the last time. The Duke's cause had become political, with support and opposition drawing up on party lines. Previously he had been able to win the necessary permission on the strengths of logical argument alone. Now he had to learn how to play the political game.

Logic would still have a part to play however. Party discipline at this time was still a malleable beast. Many of those whose approval he would need to win were those with considerable economic stakes and self-interest could be relied upon to sway some waverers if it was pitched correctly. Parliament was a fair reflection of the country as a whole, being divided between those who wanted to keep things as they were and those who were looking towards a bright new future. The Duke and his rustic companion represented the two human faces of that future. Presented together, were they a phenomenon to be embraced or threatening outsiders who deserved to be blackballed?

The Duke, Gilbert and Brindley travelled separately, with the latter arriving on 14 January. Once settled in his London townhouse, the Duke wasted no time. He decided to employ a high-risk strategy. For a number of reasons he couldn't afford the delay a long drawn-out session would bring. His subsequent actions showed him to be a shrewd tactician.

The more cynical Brindley meanwhile settled in for a long haul. Although he had been to London before, his previous visits had been purposeful and mercifully short – not open-ended like this one. The big city was not a place Brindley would have enjoyed, constraining as it was on his time and his timetable, for the list of people demanding a part of his attention was growing and he was stuck in the dirt, noise and stench of London while he could have been on moorland or by open water surveying a fresh problem.

Whether to calm him down or as a distraction, Gilbert and his wife offered to take him to see Garrick play Richard III at the theatre. This was, quite literally, to prove to be the embodiment of the culture shock he must have been experiencing at the time. He got so involved in the play and worked up in its drama that he spent the following week in bed in a state of agitation, his journals simply recording 'Not well' and 'Ill', until he eventually emerged on the following Sunday to go to church, no doubt in search of more traditional certainties. Brindley was never to attend the theatre again.

Once again, the Duke made sure that Brindley was paid well to be kept available, earning a steady seven and six a day as a retainer for his trouble, although Brindley could probably have quite easily have earned similar amounts back on his home turf doing things he would much rather be doing. Seeing as he was in London anyway, Brindley appears to have decided to make the most of it. As he was, after all, going to be speaking before Parliament he decided to rig himself out in some new clothes, recording in his journal that he spent £1 1s 8d on new britches, two guineas on a waistcoat and six shillings on some new shoes, a week's worth of retainer in total.

So-called 'starvationers' semi-submerged at the mouth of Worsley Delph. (Courtesy of The
Waterways Archive)

It would be understandable if Brindley had felt some nervousness as he prepared to attend the Parliamentary Committee. The longer they had stayed in London the clearer it had become that the Bill, despite the many fine arguments in favour of it, could well be defeated. Much depended upon how persuasive Brindley could be. The more lobbying the Duke did the clearer it became that Brindley was the fulcrum upon which the whole enterprise was balanced – and that the difference between success and failure was a fine one.

Not a man used to public speaking or playing to the crowd, Brindley's footsteps must have echoed with all the resonance of an executioner as he paced the long hallway towards the Committee Room. He had spent some time holed up with the Duke's legal team rehearsing the arguments for and against the canal. Whilst it was unlikely that Brindley would be challenged on some of the bigger issues, the Committee would be keen to hear his explanation for some of the new technology his canal was using. This element of the enterprise was completely uncharted territory and to his challengers was seen as the Duke's Achilles' Heel.

That Brindley could be persuasive there can be in little doubt, certainly when convinced that he was right. During the course of his career he had on many occasions deployed convincing rhetoric and arguments to change the minds of both masters and clients. After all, wasn't it he who had persuaded the Duke himself to change the course of his proposed canal and build the largest aqueduct in the country? His reasoning came more from the heart than through the rational world of plans and papers. Much rode upon his getting the balance between them right.

Although no record of the session remains, a number of anecdotes have passed into Brindley folklore that suggest that the questioning did indeed focus more on the mechanics of the canal and its technical feasibility. One of the doubters' greatest concerns was basic: why was it that the canal didn't simply leak as soon as water was put in it?

On being told that the answer lay in 'puddling', Committee members asked for an explanation. Preferring a practical explanation to a speech, Brindley asked for some clay and water to be brought into the room. Using the clay he fashioned a channel and poured some water into it. It duly leaked. He then took some clay and sand and mixed it together – 'puddling' it – which he again formed into a channel. This time the water stayed in.

Perhaps the most infamous of Brindley's practical demonstrations was that involving a cheese. Asked for more details on a certain type of bridge, Brindley is said to have left the room and bought a round of cheese. He then produced the pocket-knife he always carried from his coat and cut the cheese into two equal halves, turning them to rest along their flat side to represent the tops of two columns. Again using a mixture of clay and water he illustrated 'how I form a watertight trunk to carry water over rivers and valleys wherever they cross the path of the canal'.

A final anecdote deserves repeating, concerning locks. Although the principles behind locks were well established in Europe they remained a curiosity in England. To date Brindley had yet to build a lock on his canal, and throughout his career he resorted to them only when he had to. On being asked by the Committee to explain how a lock worked Brindley is said to have got down on his hands and knees and, extracting the stick of chalk he also always kept about him, even it seems in his new waistcoat, he provided his explanation through a diagram he drew on the Committee Room floor. The Honourable Members were, it seems, satisfied.

Finding answers to some of the more general objections to the canal was the Duke's job. Armed with a small team of advisers he engaged upon a series of letter campaigns, lobbying Members of Parliament with arguments in favour of his scheme. The day after Brindley spoke the Duke followed up swiftly with 200 letters, which in a time before photocopying machines must have been a task to produce.

The arguments against them were not strong, being more to do with conserving the status quo than substantive challenges to the principles of the project. Quite understandably, many of the landowners present objected to having the canals cut through their property, even though the Bill would provide for statutory compensation.

Although the Duke was offering to build stone bridges, the thought of slicing through ancient field systems was something many sought to avoid. Who was to say that cattle would use these bridges? The whole idea of having one's personal property usurped in favour of some unidentified wider social gain must have been anathema to many of the old guard. Land was for growing things, not to service a distant unvisited metropolis.

Searching for a killer punch, the opposition deployed the national interest in an attempt to whip up patriotic fervour against the canal. Wasn't England a maritime nation? Hadn't history shown that the skills and fortitude of its sailors were the very bedrock of the country's greatness? If the canals displaced sailors from the rivers a vital source of those skills would be lost. The art of manoeuvring on water would essentially become deskilled.

Water rights also came up. Wouldn't the proposed canal drain water away from the rivers, leading to droughts in dry years and preventing necessary irrigation? Although water conservation was and remains a real issue with canals, in this particular case the Duke was able to point out that the entire stretch of the canal would be supplied with water from his mines at Worsley. This was despite Brindley's response at one of the Parliamentary sessions when he was asked what the purpose of rivers was. Rather undiplomatically he had replied bluntly: 'to feed navigable canals'.

The Mersey & Irwell Navigation Company also proved to be ready to come back fighting from its attempts to buy the Duke off with concessions. Why was a new canal needed at all? The Navigation could do everything the canal could do, not least when one considered that the two ran parallel for much of their course. What was more, they claimed, the canal would drain water from their Navigation, and anyway, one of the reasons that investors had backed the Navigation and would back further improvements to it was some kind of protection from Parliament of its monopoly.

These arguments too could be countered, and the Duke wasted no time in doing so. Again showing some political acumen, the Duke spotted and exploited some of the latent hostility that had grown up around the Navigation Company over the years as they had squeezed their advantage mercilessly.

The Duke also played the manure card again, offering to carry manure free for the whole length of his canal. He also pointed out that the canal could not draw water from the Navigation as it was consistently higher than it across its length. As for damaging the commercial prospects of the Navigation Company, well, wasn't it Parliament's duty to promote the interests of the people, not a small handful of shareholders?

As the Duke became tied up with meetings, so did Brindley, although his meetings were with clients and potential clients, the businessman in him displaying a perfect willingness to further his commercial interests even when he was in the retained pay of the Duke. One such discussion involved Brindley advising on some salt works in Droitwich and a mill in Cheshire.

With more letters issued, the day of the first vote approached. The Duke issued a further 250 letters two days before the Bill was to be heard. An eight-hour debate, starting at three in the afternoon, followed on 26 February with the House eventually dividing to vote at eleven. As predicted, Members split on roughly party lines, but as the Members went through the lobbies it would have been impossible to gauge which way the vote was going to go.

For a desperate few minutes the Duke, Gilbert and Brindley, as well as the rest of the Duke's retinue, would have had to wait while the tellers did their work. Below them the empty chamber of the House would have been silent except for the occasional creaking of wood or the echo of a distant cough. With the cut and thrust of the debate removed as a distraction, those in the gallery would have become aware of the unpleasant odours of London's streets outside and of a certain coldness in the air.

The tellers returned with their verdict: for the Duke, 127; against, 98; a majority for the Duke of twenty-nine. It was enough, but the battle wasn't over yet. The Duke swept out of the chamber and with barely a rest to celebrate put into action a further 250 letters on details of the Bill. The following day the proposed legislation was gone through clause by clause, with the majority on subsequent votes sometimes as low as nineteen. Although there were

This view from Brindley's final resting place looks out over the land where the Golden Hill Colliery, from which much of his fortune derived, once stood.

some modifications the tide of opinion was now clear and the Bill passed through all its stages, eventually going through the Lords on 10 March without opposition. By this point Brindley was almost in despair at his enforced incarceration in the city, his frustration seething through in the entry in his journal that records: 'From setting out of Lancashire to this day is nine weeks.' It is almost possible to sense an exclamation mark at the end of this statement.

Lord Strange, the Duke's main opponent, was said to be 'sick with grief' with the passing of the Act. Perhaps he understood the nature of the transformation the House had now unleashed. With the principles of canal building tested and passed, the Duke's Bill would be the first of many, leading to irrevocable change in how the country looked and operated. It was, he might perhaps have ruminated, the end of an era.

★ ★ ★ ★ ★ ★ ★ ★ ★ ★

More appropriately, it was the beginning of another. For Brindley it came not a moment too soon. He had spent too long in the capital, and although his contribution to the debate may have been significant, perhaps even pivotal, he must have suffered much of the frustration of a movie actor on set, spending much more time waiting than performing.

He left as soon as he could, but was immediately given a practical example of the need for a fresh approach to the country's transport infrastructure when his mare, which had been inadequately exercised in London, seemed to have some kind of collapse, or perhaps she fell foul of a rut in the road. Whichever, she 'lost ye use of her limes [limbs]' and further progress was slow. Brindley eventually reached Congleton six days after leaving London, pausing for a couple of days to do a little maintenance work on the gearing of the silk mill there, before heading straight back to Worsley.

There he met up again with Gilbert, who had set out from London as soon as it had become clear that the Act would pass. The two had known each other for three years by then and had probably built up a sense of mutual respect, although that didn't mean they had to like one another.

This relationship was central to the success of the Duke's scheme and it was one he worked hard to preserve. Both men were creative and highly motivated, although there was one crucial distinction between them: Gilbert was ultimately an employee, whereas Brindley was a free agent. This allowed Brindley to exercise his independence when he felt he needed to, even if this meant deserting the work on the canal to meet other client needs and must have proved a useful safety valve when the pressure began to mount, as it assuredly must have at times.

Gilbert, however, was stuck with living and breathing the canal project. In the Duke's absence he was effectively in charge, and had the power, probably more implicit than exercised, to demand that things were done in a way that satisfied him, even if this meant crossing swords with Brindley. Both men of course were effectively overseers rather than labourers, and considerable latitude would have existed for each to influence the work of each others' gangs of workers by their mere presence on site, offering countless opportunities for mischief making.

More than once this lead to friction, and the Duke often found himself in the role of young conciliator to his two key men. One incident in particular stands out as an example of the tensions between the men when Gilbert's stallion broke into the paddock of Brindley's beloved mare and got her in foal. Livid, Brindley accused Gilbert of letting it happen on purpose, a claim that festered into such a simmering row between the men that the Duke was forced to intervene. Things got so bad that Gilbert's brother Thomas had to ride over from Trentham with his eldest son Tom and drink Brindley stupid at the Cock Inn at Gorshill to calm him down. As Brindley's journal wryly records, he 'stayed all night'.

Although this spat might seem trivial to us today, that there was some kind of continuing friction between the two men seems likely. Perhaps part of the explanation for this can be found in their different working styles. Gilbert was said to be a collaborator, a communicator, good with people and used to working in partnership with others. Brindley on the other hand was the archetypal loner, with his brooding contemplations, retirements to bed and pronouncements of unchallengeable certainty when he was happy he had found a solution to a problem.

Equally, it is possible that the tension between the two men was more a case of likes repelling. Both were creative and demanded high standards. They may even have been competitive in the extent to which they liked to see these standards applied. If either spotted a flaw in the works of the other they would almost certainly have wasted no time in pointing it out. Like a feuding married couple, as soon as the other was out of sight they would have rearranged the furniture to their own satisfaction, complaining that the other never did things properly. Against this background, it is possible to view their joint trip to the theatre in London in a fresh light.

Add to this the stresses that both were working under and perhaps a growing resentment on the part of Gilbert that Brindley, a man he had introduced to the Duke, seemed to be gradually assuming all the available glory for the works as they progressed. It has been suggested that Gilbert was a quiet man, modest and unassuming. Whilst this may have been the case, it would take the grace of a saint not to have felt some resentment towards Brindley.

What was more, as time went on, Brindley quite clearly benefited materially from his new position, whereas Gilbert remained simply an employee, albeit a well-rewarded one with a salary of £200 a year, although this increased to £300 when the Duke could finally afford it. Although generous – remember the Duke spent some time living off only £400 himself – as time went on Brindley would continually outstrip Gilbert in the material stakes, even though Gilbert proved to be an astute businessman and became involved in a variety of different enterprises and by no means died a pauper.

If these suppositions are true, then they would not have been the only ill-sorted couple in history to work well as a double act. It seems reasonable to suggest that their relationship was creative more often than it was destructive, punctuated by the occasional spectacular flare up, usually precipitated by Brindley. That they often worked well together is indisputable. Indeed, as we have seen, it can be difficult to be certain exactly who was the prime thinker behind many of the main achievements of the Bridgewater Canal, including parts of the Barton Aqueduct.

Elsewhere there were clear lines of distinction between them. Each cultivated and jealously protected their own spheres of influence. A clear example of this is the pumping machinery at Worsley; a pivotal part of the whole design, for without a steady supply of water the canal was nothing more than a gigantic ditch. Brindley it was who designed and built a form of steam engine to pump the water out, something Gilbert was quite happy to acknowledge he didn't understand at all.

Worsley Monument is all that remains of the tower that stood over the works in the village, its bell tolling the rhythm of the workers' day.

In true Brindley style this was no simple replication of existing technology but an improvement. Again he used wood to make both the cylinder and the chains and the contraption was said to be built for £150, against the £500 normally reckoned at the time for a machine of similar power. With this success Brindley seems to have closed the book on steam engines, although quite what he would have achieved if he could have capitalised on his learning in this field is anyone's guess.

The workings inside the mines however were Gilbert's domain, one which Brindley wisely steered clear of. By the time of his death, some years after Brindley, Gilbert had supervised the channelling of over forty miles of underground channels, a distance that superseded the entire length of the canal itself. What was more, they existed on four different levels over 100 yards apart, and shortly after his death were connected by an underground inclined plane with two parallel wagonways each capable of holding a starvationer. Throughout this time Gilbert, like Brindley, was constantly innovating, one example being the use of sluices to 'wash' the starvationers down their channels. Using this device, boats would be held behind a temporary dam until there was a sufficient head of water to propel them down the course, riding the wave like a surfer.

Over time the relationship between these two men probably matured into one of solid mutual respect. Brindley even brought Gilbert into his share of the Golden Hill Colliery, the eventual success of which would have gone some way to helping to alleviate any sense of aggrievement over the relative material rewards each had gained from the canal. In time, despite remaining in the Duke's service for the rest of his working life, Gilbert made enough to buy the Clough Hall estate near Kidsgrove for himself and his family.

The reality was that each member of the triumvirate brought their own skills, but each was sufficiently knowledgeable about aspects of each other's responsibilities, and had sufficiently strong personalities to do something about it, for some friction to be inevitable. The Duke's forte was his political acumen and negotiating skills, which allowed him to buy the land they needed, to cope with competitors and put a positive 'spin' on the whole project in the minds of people whose opinion mattered.

Gilbert's contribution was in the management of the mines and the supervision of the building of the canal, including the burden of much of the day-to-day decision making for both this enterprise and the rest of the estate. This role also involved managing and paying the workmen. One example of his natural skill in this area occurred when he noticed that his Worsley-based men were returning late to work after going home for lunch. On being told that they often missed the single chime from the works clock at one o'clock he arranged for the clock to chime thirteen, a tradition the bell in the church continues to this day.

Brindley it was who provided both specific interventions and inspiration, as well as strategic vision and belief. His particular strength was anything to do with the management of water. The Duke himself had once commented that 'water is the best of friends, but the worst of enemies' and it was this conundrum that Brindley helped to resolve.

This common understanding of, and respect for, each other's skills was about to prove critical. If it had been forged in the fire of getting the canal to and beyond Barton it was about to be proved in the inferno that was follow as the Duke set out to implement the powers Parliament had now granted him.

seven

Money Like Water

The race was on to complete the canal and nothing could be allowed to stop it. The potential of the Duke's ideas had now been exposed to anyone with the imagination to use them for themselves. Failure to exploit his position would lead inevitably to the Duke losing all of the advantages his boldness had gained him. Unfortunately for him, his precarious position was well known and it is hardly surprising that some decided to turn it to their advantage.

The picturesque town of Lymm in Cheshire is today a small haven of the county set, complete with shops selling horse tack and ammunition, on the outskirts of the less delicate delights of Warrington. Its inhabitants clearly have a keen eye for the accumulation of wealth, an attribute that would appear to be deeply rooted, as is ably demonstrated by an incident during the urgent second phase of the building of the Bridgewater Canal.

Brindley's survey had identified a route that took the canal through the garden of a cottage belonging to one of Lymm's poorer inhabitants. The small garden consisted of a single pear tree. The fruit from this tree must have been particularly sweet because the owner managed to hold out for a price of thirty guineas for that plot, an exorbitant sum equivalent to an artisan's annual income, and probably enough to elevate the owner in Lymm's social hierarchy.

Such incidents were to become all too common, but they could not be allowed to obstruct progress. Brindley concentrated on the route towards the Mersey, whilst Gilbert supervised the final stretch into Manchester. The Duke meanwhile got involved in land purchases, spending money like it was going out of style. Thirty guineas for a garden was chickenfeed when compared with the £40,000 he spent on the land where the warehouses and docks were going to be built in Manchester. From this point on matters of finance were to dominate the Duke's life.

The story that follows is a tribute either to one man's far-sightedness or his foolhardiness. Evidence for the former, and for the Duke's canniness with money, would be the bargain £4,200 he paid for the land that would eventually become the docks at the Liverpool end of the canal, even before he had parliamentary permission to extend the canal east. For years this purchase was kept secret, not even appearing in John Gilbert's Worsley accounts until 1783, with the land leased to tenants while it awaited its intended purpose.

This secrecy is particularly revealing given the fastidious nature of John Gilbert and the normal accuracy of his accounts. Some have even gone so far as to suggest that the Duke had always envisaged three stages to deliver his master plan. This probably grants the man a subtlety he did not possess when one takes into account his relatively modest intellect. What there can be no doubt of, however, is his growing obsession with the canal and what it represented. Whether this was because it gave him a purpose and was, effectively, in lieu of a marriage and family (he was said to be openly contemptuous of women following his dealings with the Duchess of Argyle) we cannot be sure. Alternatively it could be that the beast grew out of proportion before he could do much about it. He was in too deep to pull out, and getting in deeper every day.

Estimating the costs of a canal was also an extremely imprecise science. Because it was funded from the deep pockets and ducal reputation of one man it didn't have any business plan, cash flow forecast or budget. Obstacles were overcome when they cropped up and were rarely predictable. The whole enterprise was built upon an idea underpinned by faith. The Act of Parliament had itself been obtained on a fairly rudimentary survey, which wouldn't even deserve the name today, being more of an opinion of feasibility. No borings were made to test underlying geology. No market research was undertaken to prove the potential markets.

If the Duke had looked to Brindley for an estimate of costs he would have been wasting his time. As for many great engineers, the excitement for Brindley lay in the challenge not the cost, a subject that would have bored him. For much of the building of the Bridgewater Canal Brindley didn't even claim a reasonable return for his own effort. If he couldn't manage his own finances it is unlikely that his skills as a project estimator would have been up to much.

By 1762 the Duke was already £27,701 in debt and that year was forced to do the one thing the aristocracy only ever do in extremis – sell land. Parts of his estate around Whitchurch in Shropshire were disposed of at around this time for the sum of £5,548, not enough to solve his problems, but enough to finance a mile or two more of his prized canal. This sale should be viewed against the backdrop of purchases elsewhere however, notably around the mine so that Gilbert could extend his channels ever deeper. A more generous interpretation therefore was that this sale represented a redistribution of his land portfolio. It also provides further evidence for those prepared to present the case for the Duke as a far-sighted operator.

The Duke was later to say that the canal cost him 2,000 guineas a mile, although subsequent estimates have varied. The sum generally agreed for the total cost was £220,000. This was an inconceivable amount for one man to carry, and not even a Duke could shoulder it alone, so what were his options?

One would have been to create a joint-stock company, but this approach was still out of favour following the South Sea Bubble earlier in the century, and anyway would have involved some dilution of control, something the Duke was keen to hang onto, as shown by the way he was holding the Liverpool card to his chest. Besides, even if he had pursued this route it is doubtful how popular an investment the canal would have been.

Although few could deny the Duke his daring and the sheer vision of the canal, the whole enterprise, from the very idea of an artificial waterway to the supplying of coal and food to the masses of Manchester, was one founded on theory rather than proven practice. Furthermore, it was well known that the Mersey & Irwell Navigation had never paid a dividend (although rather conveniently for them in the escalating war of words between the two projects it started to do so in 1764), and from any potential investor's point of view the Duke had handicapped himself by his rash promises on the price at which he would sell his coal even if it did ever get to Manchester.

Instead, the Duke did the only thing he could do – like a daring player of Monopoly he mortgaged the properties he didn't need in order to raise cash to buy those he did. Evidence for this includes a detailed map of the Duke's lands drawn up in 1764 and used as a mortgage document. At the same time he raised funds through the issuing of bonds, and lots of them. Each of these was a document in its own right, allowing him to retain the level of secrecy as to his true position the project demanded. As with all large capital projects, maintaining confidence was essential and in this the Duke was a master.

Each bond would state clearly the amount being lent, the name of the lender and the rate of guaranteed interest being offered, which typically would vary between four and eight per cent. Critically, these bonds were redeemable by the lender at will, piling on the risk to the Duke any sudden loss of confidence would entail. For the many years it took to complete the canal the Duke lived every day on the edge of financial ruin.

Just how precarious his position had become is illustrated by the incident when he offered a bill of £500 to a Manchester Bank and was refused – an extreme reaction towards a peer of the realm. During this time the Duke continued to give Brindley his full confidence. What he wanted he normally got, not that Brindley was a man who would accept compromise. If the Duke had needed support in the need for economy he would have more likely turned to Gilbert, who always had a keen eye for the cost of the canal, as illustrated by his conversion of the lime beneath the canal into a waterproof mortar.

To Gilbert fell the responsibility for shouldering the day-to-day impact of the Duke's impecuniousness. Fridays were particularly fraught for Gilbert as this was the day the men had to be paid. At one point he was to be found raising cash off his tenants and redistributing it amongst the canal workers. Any thought that this might have caused resentment can be balanced by the fact that the canal workers would often go short or even defer their pay altogether. The hardship this must have caused is hard to imagine at a time when life was very much a hand-to-mouth affair. Everyone, it seems, was in this together with the Duke.

One story goes that things got so bad that when he was out on his rounds one day he came across a gentlemen with a fine horse who, after a short chat, offered to swap his mount for Gilbert's. As Gilbert's horse was clearly inferior to the stranger's he agreed, only to find that when he reached the inn that he had unknowingly traded with a gentleman of the road, a highwayman, on the run.

Between them Gilbert and the Duke thought up a number of schemes to squeeze some kind of revenue out of the as yet unfinished canal. One of these was the planting of quick growing trees in the bogs at Trafford Moss, which could be harvested and sold as drying frames to the cotton dyers in Manchester. Although the revenue this provided would have been meagre it was at least something, and the trees were helpful in stabilising the banks of the canal at that point. In another example the Duke devised the idea of draining the canal in winter into his own meadows so that he could grow the hay he needed to feed the mules that pulled his boats.

By 1765 the Duke's debts had risen to £60,879 and counting. To put this in perspective, gross profit from the mine that year was £5,230 but he spent £2,468 in wages and materials.

At the height of the canals as a transport artery, whole families would live together in the tiny cabins, leaving the bulk of the boat to carry their cargo. (Courtesy of Manchester Central Library)

To this should be added a further £1,000 income from lime and passengers on the pleasure craft that had begun to ply his canal. Incredibly, or perhaps encouraged by the fact that he had an income at all, around this time the Duke decided, with due bravado, to build a new Hall. His confidence in eventual success must have been rock solid.

Almost immediately after gaining his Act of Parliament the canal became a war, being fought on three fronts: the mine, the Manchester arm and the men striking out towards Liverpool. Once the coal left the mine the principle of a 'flat' waterway was maintained throughout the length of the canal, that is to say that it remained at the same height throughout, entirely without locks. If this meant taking a meandering route in order to skirt a natural obstacle then so be it. Elsewhere, if it meant carving a passage out of solid rock, draining a marsh or building yet more aqueducts or bridges then these too would be achieved.

Other than its status as pioneer, the Bridgewater Canal was unique in that it was completely independent of other waterways, carved out of the soil by man rather than a refinement of a natural course. To this day it has no locks. This is not to say that lock technology was not available, the Duke would have seen them on his Grand Tour in Europe and the original plan at Barton was to take the canal down to the river and up again through locks; simply that Brindley seemed to have an aversion to them. In fact in Brindley's day the canal did have locks, but only at its very end in Runcorn, where the waterway was delivered down to the Mersey, but these have since become disused, a blank wall decorated with graffiti proclaiming the end of the modern line.

Having got the nod from Parliament, completion of the Liverpool branch was largely Brindley's responsibility and he was back reconnoitring its course within weeks of returning from London after his performance before the Parliamentary Committee. The remainder of the year was spent catching up on outstanding affairs, as well as the first of what would turn out to be numerous commissions to survey other possible waterways, including one for a navigation from Chester to Shrewsbury and another from Rotherham to Doncaster, moves that no doubt fed the Duke's anxiety.

The Liverpool branch was by some degree greater than the cut through into Manchester, not only in terms of scale but also the complexity of the land they had to go through. Significantly the canal would have to go over the Irwell again and had to cope with a number of streams that would need to be channelled if Brindley's golden rule about not mingling water from different sources was to be upheld. Bridges and aqueducts would be needed and the bogs at Trafford Moss and Sale Moor were a particular challenge. These were said to be so impassable that cattle sometimes vanished entirely into the depths.

Before Sale however, Brindley had to cross the Mersey, a challenge it took him most of 1763 to complete. This required another aqueduct, so soon after the completion of Barton. Although a smaller construction this was still significant, as his journal of November of that year records: 'settled about the size of the arch over the river Marsee [Mersey] to be 66 foot span and rise 164 feet'.

Building the bridge occupied him full time, with daily entries in his journal for dinner at the Bull Inn at eight pence. For the first time Brindley started to record his activities in his journals in terms of 'forenoon' and 'afternoon' to keep track of everything he was doing. As well as crossing the Mersey he was also involved in supervising activities at Cornbrook near the terminus at Manchester, frequently ferrying between the two. Throughout, his role was multi-faceted, with his records detailing work involving masonry, paving, carpentry and drain work.

Once again this period saw growing stress amongst the principle players in this drama. Not only was the Duke scrabbling around for fresh money but many of the incidents between Brindley and Gilbert already described took place around this time. At one point Brindley became so angry with Gilbert poaching his men that he sent a note round by messenger cutting off further contact between them, or as he put it 'no more society'.

Brindley also became highly agitated about his new bridge, returning to his old habit of retiring to bed when the heat was on, or in this case, when the floods were rising. During November heavy rains had raised the level of the canal and threatened to overwhelm his new bridge, not yet bedded in. His journals record how he 'lay in bed till noon, floode and rain … the water in Longford Brook within six inches of the high of the junction of the weir'. In the end the waters subsided and work could continue, but it had been a close call.

By this time the Manchester branch had reached Trafford and Gilbert was busy extending the mines. Meanwhile, the threat the canal represented was becoming all too apparent and those most likely to lose out were marshalling their defences for a last act of defiance, offering to lower their prices in an attempt to stifle the Duke while he was still vulnerable. They failed, and the Navigation eventually offered to sell itself to the Duke for £13,000, which although a considerable sum was nothing compared with the other sums he was spending at the time. He doesn't seem to have been tempted however, as events were clearly turning his way.

As the canal progressed, growing confidence in its viability allowed the Duke to convince others that he was developing a working concern and that it was a backable proposition. Rather than exploit this by issuing shares the Duke instead raised a fresh loan of £25,000 from his family banker Sir Francis Child. The Duke's aversion to diluting his control of the canal has already been commented upon but a more practical reason lay behind his continuing need to go it alone.

As we have seen, given the scale of the enterprise and the fact that it cut indiscriminately through numerous estates, the Duke had been forced to go to Parliament for permission to build the canal. Such permission was usually contingent on a proposal, nominally at least, pursing the public good. As such there was a veneer of altruism in this first canal that meant that the brazen commercial pursuit of profit might not have looked good. Although this illusion was shattered by those that followed, the Duke was breaking new ground and had to tread carefully.

Even this loan wasn't enough however, and the Duke continued to seek investors wherever he could find them, even if it meant mixing business with pleasure. Horse-racing remained a hangover from his dandy days and as a pressure valve from the stress of building his canal he would still go to the races for a break.

If he went for relaxation then he would have failed, as he found it impossible to get away from thoughts about his canal and he would corner anyone he could with tales of its superiority over rivers and the benefits it would bring, adding a sting in the tail with an offer to invest in this marvellous opportunity. Quite how many friends he retained from this time it is difficult to imagine, after a while it couldn't have been surprising if word got around the race course that the Duke was about and visitors who knew him would be planning how to avoid him. Gambling on horses might have been one thing but on artificial waterways, well that was another altogether.

As the canal progressed the Duke had literally hundreds of men working for him, or more accurately for Brindley and Gilbert. One contemporary observer of the works commented that he had counted at least 400 men working along a 200 yard stretch – and that was on a Sunday. The numbers involved were more than either man could effectively oversee, especially as Brindley was still free to disappear and do other things, sometimes for days on end. As such it is not surprising that systems of foremen and gangs, normally organised around fifty at a time, developed.

Through the typically Brindley-esque approach of trial and error these men effectively invented the art of being a navigator, or navvy. Most were simple labourers, although a high proportion were also skilled bricklayers, carpenters and blacksmiths, all adapting their skills to meet the new demands. Less skilled men had probably been thrown off the land and had little alternative other than the workhouse. Once they started to travel with the canal however, they would have lost even that option along with the benefit of having a home parish. Once brought into the canal net it seemed that your fate was tied to it.

Probably unable to swim, they laboured hard, taking their families with them, so that a new canal would advance down its route like a slow army, loud and rhythmic, chaotic yet purposeful. Temporary villages would be created with campfires, common areas and children playing. The impact of an oncoming tide of navvies coming towards your land must have been phenomenal. Sweeping up all before them like a plague of locusts, they would have been loud, arrogant and threatening. It's not surprising that locals often objected to their arrival and riots requiring the intervention of the local militiamen were not uncommon.

Brindley soon acquired his most trusted lieutenants from amongst this motley crew, often referring to them by name in his journals with nicknames such as 'Black David' or 'Bill o'Toms'. Those who chose to become navvies tended to be drawn from the diaspora of working life, those who had rejected conventional ways of earning a living or had struggled to find a trade that would suit.

Footloose and hard working, they were ideal fodder for Brindley and his demands. Some were heavy drinkers, others total abstainers. Some were men of God, others dissenters. Many probably saw a little of themselves in his sometimes eccentric ways, and a bond of mutual trust often built up between them. This sense of another class later transferred itself to those who chose to make a living from the completed canals, with boatmen regarded by some as little more than water-bound gypsies.

So where did all these men come from? It was symptomatic of the changing economics of the country that the labour force became much more mobile during the eighteenth century. Apprentices, servants, itinerant farm workers turned out by the enclosures, immigrants from Ireland, discharged soldiers and general journeymen all contributed to the feeling of a country on the move, even if the act of moving was difficult and for most involved walking. Farm workers could expect to change jobs on an annual basis, offering themselves for hire at district hiring fares. For those with some kind of skill or a sense of adventure being a navvy wasn't such a bad option.

Meanwhile the money troubles to pay all these navvies continued. Not only was the Duke financing the cutting of a two-headed canal, but Gilbert was merrily cutting into the hillside to get at the coal and building a small navy of boats to carry it out. From being a fairly modest village living off arable farming, mainly oats, barley and corn, with the coming of the third Duke, Worsley became the Georgian equivalent of a significant industrial estate. In time it employed 3,000 people and included a timber yard, a boat yard, warehousing, lime quarrying and a lead works. It was in effect one of the world's first manufacturing towns and its status as such was recently recognised when it was placed on a short list to become a World Heritage Site.

Observing the hive of activity before him in 1773, Josiah Wedgwood remarked that Worsley had 'the appearance of a considerable seaport', despite being thirty miles from the coast. By this time the town had become a tourist attraction in its own right attracting minor royalty and even the French philosopher Jean Jacques Rousseau. Becoming increasingly complex over time, the town became a conglomerate of activity and interests, some of which Gilbert himself had a direct investment in, such as a lead-pencil and grate-polish factory called Gilbert and Jackson.

All this activity had as its source the mine entrance hidden away in a corner of the town down a spur of the canal. Two small gaping semi-circular mouths either side of a sheer rock cliff would, as today, spew a constant stream of dark gold water into the canal. Above the cliff sat the town's church, as if keeping watch on the work of Mammon. At regular intervals the atmosphere would be rent with the terrifying screech of air being sent down into the bowels of the cavern from the bellows up above. On a tiny island between the two entrances a small army of overseers and foremen would be milling about, barking orders and counting boats in and out of the mine. Hidden from human eye would be the deep workings of the mines themselves, a complex labyrinth of roughly hewn rock and bricked up arches echoing to the sounds of picks, men and horses, while the boats plied their business largely in silence.

Within a decade Worsley became a microcosm of how industrialisation would develop in the manufacturing centres across the country, centres that the canal network would surely link and thereby lubricate the process of trade. The grate-polish factory, for example, used raw materials shipped in from a plumbago or black-lead mine in the Lake District. This in turn was part-owned by the Duke and other associates, all of whom held shares. The development of Worsley would have proved a haven for would-be entrepreneurs, and following the eventual success of the canal both Gilbert, the Duke, and to some extent Brindley, proved to be adept entrepreneurs.

This Grail was still a little way off however, although it became easier over time to imagine how things might develop. In the meantime things had got so bad for the Duke that at one point he was forced to hide from the local rector chasing his tithes. Like his friends at the racecourse it was a case of 'not if I see you first' as the two dodged about the town, the rector searching, the Duke hiding. Eventually the rector succeeded in running his prey to ground in a sawpit and the Duke, showing amazing good humour, laughed at his predicament and promised to pay up.

Eventually things came to a head and a council of war was called at a local inn. The scene may well bring to mind that with the three vultures in Disney's 'Jungle Book', each mournfully asking 'What are we going to do now then?' as they contemplated their dilemma. A canal more than half built but no money left to finish it. Their pipes lit, their glasses full, the Duke is said to have turned to Brindley and asked: 'Well Brindley, how are we to get at the money for finishing this canal?' Brindley, as was his way, went silent, pondering his response, before sucking on his pipe and rejoining 'Well Duke, I can't tell; I only know that if the money can be got I can finish the canal and that it will pay well.' The Duke responded to this observation with a wry 'Ay, but where are we to get the money?' and probably brought his glass back to his lips.

Brindley simply repeated his previous answer whereupon the party fell into a gloomy despair until Brindley chirped up once more, 'Don't mind Duke; don't be cast down; we are sure to succeed after all', and in so doing quite neatly summed up the relationship between the two men. It was the Duke's job to get the money, it was Brindley's to build the canal and Gilbert's to act as the conduit between the two. Thus resolved, the three men separated and carried on as before.

However bad things might have been, the Duke managed to keep a sense of humour, as well as generosity. One story told about him was that he once spotted one of his workmen going to work late one morning and stopped him to find out the reason. The workman, red eyed and patently tired, replied that his wife had given birth to twins during the night. Stumped for a response, the Duke muttered a platitude like 'Ay well, we've to have what the good Lord sends us', to which the workman replied 'Ay, I notice he sends al't babbies to our house and al't brass to yours'. No doubt amused, the Duke tipped the man a generous guinea, a sum he could barely afford.

The Duke also kept his spirits up with rides on his boats, never tiring of taking a trip out on the water to survey his liquid monument. He used these trips to inspect the work going

1 The somewhat fanciful representation of the opening of the Barton Aqueduct painted by Ford Maddox Brown and today on display in Manchester City Hall. (Courtesy of Manchester City Council)

2 A small remnant of the original aqueduct can be seen in the corner of the modern version of Barton.

3 Working steamboats NB *President* and NB *Kildare* still ply the system today and give a good idea of the noises and smells associated with post horse-pulled boating.

4 One of Brindley's journals and his level, as displayed at the Brindley Mill Museum in Leek. (Courtesy of Brian Moran, Brindley Mill)

5 *Above:* The twin entrances to Worsley Delph are scarcely visible today, but in Brindley and Gilbert's day they would have been the heart of a massive industrial enterprise.

6 *Right:* Perhaps ironically, the Duke of Bridgewater was buried on his estates in Ashridge, Hertfordshire rather than Worsley, where a monument commemorates his achievements.

7 The Star Inn at Stone has some claims to be the oldest canal pub in the country.

8 The Staffordshire and Worcester Canal joined the Trent and Mersey Canal at Great Haywood, and the conjunction of two towpaths required a rather convoluted bridge.

9 Brindley's tunnel is barely visible today at the Harecastle's southern portal.

10 At its southern end the Harecastle seems to sneak out of the hillside unnoticed.

11 One of the distinctive bottle kilns of the Potteries, now sadly few and far between.

12 *Opposite above:* Boats lining the banks of the Oxford Canal today.

13 *Opposite below:* The lock keeper's cottage at Cropredy in Oxfordshire shows how men maintaining the canal lived quite literally above the shop.

14 Thrupp boats. Today, as in the past, boats often vie with each other in terms of decoration.

15 Nell Bridge lock on the South Oxford Canal shows the classic marriage of lock and lockkeeper's cottage.

on and would often be found popping up on site to check out how things were going. If he found something wrong, or if the men were being abused in any way, he invariably set himself the task of taking up the cause and doing something about it. All contemporary reports on the Duke's character stress his humanity and lack of 'side', referring to his happiness to mingle with his men and to intervene personally over cases of genuine hardship. His canal was, it seems, his life around this time and he visited his other houses only rarely.

But still the money was flowing out of his hands as easily as the boats floated down his waterway. Caught over a barrel, things turned from bad to worse when he had to stump up £40,000 to buy the land he needed for the docks at the Runcorn end of the canal, where it was planned to drop into the Mersey. Things had got so bad that even Brindley's ambition had to be held in check. When told of the price of this land Brindley came up with the bold suggestion that they build a bridge across the Mersey straight over to their final destination at Liverpool. Such a bridge would have made Barton look like a training exercise, being a quarter of a mile long. The Duke resisted, although what kind of language he used in doing so we do not know.

Good news finally came in 1765, the same year that HMS *Victory* was launched, with completion of the branch into Manchester, which ended at Castlefield, near where the G-Mex complex now stands. The completion of this front allowed the team to concentrate wholly on the Runcorn arm, but more importantly it immediately demonstrated the financial viability of the whole scheme. With instant effect the price of coal plummeted and there could be no doubt that the Duke some had called mad was in fact about to make a fortune.

The twin entrances to Worsley Delph are scarcely visible today, but in Brindley and Gilbert's day they would have been the heart of a massive industrial enterprise.

The Runcorn arm had by now reached Altrincham and, as the Duke had always feared, other groups were beginning to become organised. Fortunately for the Duke the leading group consisted of friends. Chief amongst these was Josiah Wedgwood, who by this time had become a great admirer, almost a groupie, of both Brindley and the Duke. Earl Gower was also prominent, as were other local MPs, with technical support offered by Hugh Henshall, a land surveyor and fellow shareholder with Brindley in the Golden Hill Colliery. This group's aim was to resurrect the idea of a canal cutting through the northern Midlands, to be called the Staffordshire canal, designed to link the salt mines of Cheshire and the potteries of Staffordshire with the port of Liverpool.

This cabal began to plot and plan, meeting sometimes together and sometimes in groups, at first warily but soon on increasingly friendly terms. They met in the archetypal smoke-filled rooms where important decisions are made, as each of them, all men, sat down, extracted a pipe from their waistcoat, and lit up, standing occasionally to consult detailed plans drawn up by Brindley, Henshall and others.

Although their meetings were probably public knowledge amongst the cognoscenti, a veneer of secrecy was maintained. Other schemes were also being discussed, principally ideas to use existing rivers such as the Weaver and the Dee to cut through to the Mersey. Although not strictly canals, proponents of these schemes represented a real threat. What was more, they would be independent of the Bridgewater.

The cabal's consultations extracted two main conclusions. The first was that the wide gauge the Duke had adopted for his canal was simply too ambitious to carry all the way to the Trent. The proposed waterway was to be nearly four times the length of the Bridgewater and didn't have the luxury of an underground water supply to feed it. What was more it was clear that locks were going to be a prominent feature of the new canal and if these were constructed to meet the width of the Bridgewater it would be both prohibitively expensive and impossible to supply with water. Instead, a gauge of seven foot was agreed, experiments with narrower craft on the Duke's canal having proved that these were acceptable.

The second agreement was perhaps more momentous. All the parties involved could see that if they worked together each canal could gain an advantage if they met at Preston Brook, four miles outside Runcorn and the Bridgewater canal's proposed meeting point with the Mersey. This would necessitate a short detour but the Duke used the fact that his canal was a reality rather than simply a proposal to negotiate an agreement that the final stretch would officially be his. By linking the two canals together everyone could appreciate that the beginnings of a network could be created – in modern parlance, an embryonic network would add value to each other's enterprise. Things were starting to get interesting.

This vision was as far-sighted as it was daring. It took the Duke a further eleven years for the link between Liverpool and Manchester to be completed, a period extended by the bitter recalcitrance of a number of landowners on the route, the most notorious of which was Sir Richard Brooke who took three years to be persuaded to give up his land at Norton Priory. The Duke also had to buy the whole of George Lloyd's Hulme Hall estates to get the land he needed to complete the Manchester terminus at a further cost of £9,000. His opponents were truly squeezing him for every last drop.

Brindley was never to see the competed canal, which finally opened four months before the Declaration of American Independence in 1776. The Duke, however, did live to enjoy the benefits of his project, something that continued to occupy his attention and exercise his sense of entrepreneurialism for the rest of his life. He continued to extend his interests in the canal and as he became more secure happily passed on the benefits of his experience to others interested in building their own. In 1795 he even returned to Parliament to get permission to extend his canal from Worsley to Leigh to link up with the Leeds and Liverpool Canal then under discussion. His place in history was secure, his debts were paid off and he could bask in the glory of his achievement.

There can be little doubt that where the Bridgewater Canal led, others followed. Its construction had proved not only the feasibility of canal building, something Brindley must take most of the credit for, but also its potential socio-economic, nay political impact. By linking Manchester and Liverpool he set these two great cities free to trade their way into greatness. From being vibrant but isolated communities, they became the hubs of local enterprise, replicating the effect that London had previously had on the south of the country in its north.

At last there was a counterweight to London's prominence, but rather than being competitive to London these cities complemented it by creating fresh sources of national wealth. An industrial engine could now crank up that would offer a contrast to the service-led consumerism of London. Decisively, the position of Liverpool meant that the products of this industry could find markets outside the country, reinforcing the country's maritime tradition by literally shipping goods to new and sometimes yet to be created markets. The fundamentals of trade and of mercantile empire had been forged.

After the success of the canal was proven the Duke quite legitimately chose to enjoy the fruits of his courage and risk. In time he became quite chubby and was said to look like his King, George III, in appearance, which is perhaps ironic seeing that he was once regarded as mad himself. He became rich and indulged a passion for art, building up what became known as the Bridgewater Collection. At one point he was to give his annual income as £110,000 and he must have been one of the handful of men in the country who was sufficiently wealthy to give £100,000 cash to the £18 million Loyalty Loan raised in 1797 by Prime Minister Pitt for the prosecution of the war against France, an expedient adopted due to the poor public finances of the time.

With the Bridgewater Canal linked irrevocably to the Duke it is fitting that when he died, without heirs, ownership of the canal and collieries passed into a trust. The provisions of this trust were so tight that it almost felt as if he was maintaining the iron grip he had exercised during his lifetime even beyond the grave. The lucky beneficiary of his will, worth around £600,000, a small fortune, was George Granville, who was appropriately enough Earl Gower's son and was later to become the First Duke of Sutherland.

Although the Duke asked to be buried at his estate at Ashridge in Hertfordshire this was only the resting place for his remains. His spirit remains to this day in Worsley, now a picturesque village rather than Georgian industrial estate, and the vein of copper-bronze water that flows through it.

★ ★ ★ ★ ★ ★ ★ ★ ★ ★

The Packet House at Worsley, with its steps from which passengers on the Duke's pleasure packet-boat would embark and disembark for trips down his new canal.

Just about the time that the Staffordshire Canal was being discussed James Brindley did something it looked like he would never do – he got married. This fact suggests a number of things about the man at this time. Not only can we assume that he had slightly more time on his hands, although this term was relative, but that he was clearly, quite justifiably, feeling bullish about his future.

He was by now a rich and successful man with the world at his feet. His expertise was being courted by the great and good and he was the part-owner of a successful colliery. A letter from Davis Dukart, an engineer and architect bemoaning the difficulties of finding suitable overseers for canal projects around this time suggested that 'Brindley has £500 per year from the Staffordshire work only… [and] does not attend one month in twelve'. Brindley had every right to feel optimistic.

His bride was Anne Henshall, sister to Hugh Henshall, Brindley's surveyor colleague and business partner. Some commentators have suggested that this was an arranged marriage, and whilst it turned out to be very convenient for Henshall, who ended up becoming Brindley's right-hand man, romantics might prefer to see it as a love match. From a modern perspective Brindley's choice and method of courtship was more than a little dubious, for Anne was barely nineteen and he was just short of fifty. He had apparently always treated her as something of a favourite during her teenage years, offering her pieces of gingerbread he kept in his jacket pocket whenever he visited Hugh.

Times were of course different then, and it is likely that rather than being outraged, or at least suspicious, as might be a modern father's instinct, it is more likely that Hugh Henshall probably encouraged this interest. As for Anne's thoughts we can only speculate, but marriage was something that would have been on the mind of a girl of nineteen and Brindley would have represented something of a catch – financially, if not physically. Marriages between older men and younger women were not unusual, although the age gap here may have raised one or two eyebrows. If convenience was indeed the motive Anne would have been encouraged by the fact that Brindley was hardly ever around and liked to keep his own company.

As for Brindley himself, he perhaps saw marriage as something that would crown his achievements. He did after all come from a Quaker background and having a family would have been something that might have fitted into his natural order of things. Perhaps he was also beginning to wonder how his talents might best be passed on to the next generation.

With success and marriage Brindley decided it was time to put down some roots and he bought the recently vacant Turnhust Hall, which was convenient not only for the colliery but also for the new project that was beginning to absorb his attention; finding a way the new Staffordshire Canal could breach the hill at Harecastle. For the first time in his life Turnhurst Hall provided Brindley with a secure family home. After five years, a first daughter was born, Ann, followed shortly afterwards by another, Susannah, although neither were destined to get to know their father.

The Hall had originally been in the ownership of the Bellot family and was said to be the last house in England to employ a family fool. In the garden there was a small summerhouse and such is the way with men and sheds, this became Brindley's den where he secreted himself away and did his planning. It was to be a space well used. Brindley had embarked upon the adventure of marriage just as he was about to enter upon the period that would set the seal upon his life and achievements.

eight

The Grand Cross

The Grand Cross was an idea that was stunning in its daring and shameless in its simplicity. It effectively mapped out a central nervous system for England's transport infrastructure. The idea was to connect the country's four main rivers, the Mersey, the Trent, the Severn and the Thames, each of which offered a path to the sea in the four corners of Liverpool, Hull, Bristol and London. Join those corners up and what you got was a cross, with the growing industrial heart of Birmingham at its intersection. Add spurs off the cross and what you got was a network, the nerves that connected to the core to make the system.

A great idea, but one whose inspiration has been disputed. Although usually attributed to James Brindley there are other claimants. Rather than investigate these, perhaps it is worthwhile discerning a pattern here. When it comes to canals there are always rivals available to contest the honour of being the first to think of each new innovation. There is a trend however, and that is the common thread of James Brindley whose name is always in the frame. This cannot be put down to mere coincidence. The Grand Cross has Brindley's name all over it – audacious but possible, challenging but expensive, it had to be his baby.

The first part of this grand plan was the Grand Trunk, the canal that had been under discussion for some time to link the Trent and the Mersey. If built, this canal would broadly describe a 'V' heading south east down from the intersection with the Duke's canal, across the flatlands of Cheshire from which it would climb nearly 400 feet to the Potteries as far as Fradley, just north of Lichfield, where it would head north east, falling 280 feet through Burton and on to Shardlow, south of Derby, where it would join the Trent. From here it would be possible to navigate by river all the way to Hull. Its name, the Grand Trunk, was derived from the fact that it would act as a main artery from which any number of connecting links could be attached. In other words, it was the spine of the Grand Cross.

As we have seen, Brindley had already been involved in some early surveying of a possible route, but this had come to nothing. This work had been followed up by a fresh route surveyed by Hugh Henshall and verified by John Smeaton, at the time one of the most eminent engineers in the land. This suggested a route that led from Longridge in the Potteries to the

The Trent & Mersey Canal continues to display regular mileposts along its route.

Mersey, a less grand idea than the Grand Trunk but one that met the needs of its main sponsors in the pottery trade.

Ideas came and went. Smeaton, for example, now a convert to the idea of canals put forward his own plan that involved a shorter link into the River Weaver. The sheer fact was the idea of the Grand Trunk was quite mind-bogglingly grandiose. If the ten miles from Worsley to Manchester had practically bankrupted the Duke of Bridgewater, imagine the concerns surrounding a link with the Potteries at a time when the viability of the Duke's canal had still to be proved.

Compared with what was now being considered, the Bridgewater was a picnic, and as such it's no surprise that more modest alternatives were considered first. Here are some thoughts that would have kept the planners awake at nights: a link from the Trent to the Mersey would require around 100 miles of waterway, to negotiate topography between the two points fully seventy-six locks would be needed (remember the Bridgewater had none except at its terminus); and most significantly, just outside Stoke stood Harecastle Hill, which the engineers were already suggesting would require a tunnel the best part of two miles long.

Despite all these objections, the longer the Duke and Brindley went on, the more it became clear to the potters of Stoke, and Josiah Wedgwood in particular, that a canal was what they needed. They were more ambivalent on the issue of whether it needed to extend to meet the Trent, first and foremost they were businessmen with a need they thought a canal could fulfil. What they lacked was the organisation, finance and sheer chutzpah of someone like Francis Egerton to make it happen. Egerton however was unique, there was no one else like him around they could recruit. Wedgwood realised that whilst between them they could probably organise themselves and raise the finance, what they lacked was the chutzpah. As time went on however, and the Bridgewater Canal showed what was possible, a potential source for that was staring them in the face.

There really was only one man for the job. They would need the vision, the expertise, and the sheer *scheming* of James Brindley. If the Bridgewater had been the result of the joint efforts of three men, The Grand Trunk was to be Brindley's masterpiece and Brindley's alone. If Brindley was the obvious choice for this task however, it was equally obvious that he was presently tied up.

In the absence of clarity various plans were put forward, with the usual interest groups lobbying their particular causes. One such were the coal merchants around the Potteries, who saw, quite legitimately, a direct threat to their trade from a canal that originated in Cheshire. The River Weaver Navigation Company, like the Mersey and Irwell before them, were equally dismayed by the idea of a competitor that ran practically parallel to their own route and put forward their alternative suggestions.

Thomas Gilbert, brother of John and perhaps slightly jealous of the acclaim his little brother had received, put forward his own plan. This linked the Trent with the Mersey, but from Josiah Wedgwood's perspective it had a fundamental flaw. In the rush towards creating a Grand Trunk it missed out the Potteries altogether. As the idea of the grander scheme began to gain ground over the more limited Staffordshire-only canal, interests at Burton-on-Trent began to make their voices heard. From their angle the obvious thing to do would be to terminate the canal in their town and to follow the Trent on from there.

They were fighting a lost cause. By 1765 one of the main lessons of the Bridgewater had been written into the canal rulebook, and it was one of Brindley's cardinal rules: never mix water from two different sources. The Bridgewater had been an arterial canal, totally man-made and independent of the vagaries of the rivers. Those proposing the Grand Trunk suggested it should be the same, convinced by a mixture of technological and commercial arguments; for like the Duke before them, they did not want their canal to become beholden to the potential charges of a third party. Despite this decision, the good burghers of Burton continued to argue their case for fully twenty years.

1765 was a seminal year for the Grand Trunk. Thomas Gilbert was persuaded at the last moment by Josiah Wedgwood to alter his plans to include the Potteries, thus winning the argument for the more ambitious project. From this point on Wedgwood decided to take a direct involvement in the scheme, no doubt to make sure that no more hare-brained ideas were introduced. At the same time James Brindley became free and a deal was struck with the Duke of Bridgewater to share the final few miles into Runcorn. All the ducks were in line. It was time to go public.

On the last but one day of that year a meeting was convened at Wolseley Bridge outside Stafford to include all those whose opinion mattered on the proposed scheme. These included the usual suspects such as Earl Gower, Wedgwood, Thomas Gilbert (who was also MP for Newcastle under Lyme) and Brindley as well as other local MPs and Lord Grey. The aim of the meeting was to convince local landowners to go along with the scheme and to drum up investment. None of those backing the scheme had pockets as deep as the Duke, and even if they did they had other interests to pursue.

Earl Gower began proceedings with what was described as 'a very sensible and elegant speech'. The man the assembled really wanted to hear though was Brindley. What he had to say would have frightened some and invigorated others. He cited the assistance he had had from John Smeaton, daring those gathered to question the integrity of their joint opinion.

For a usually contemplative man Brindley knew how to turn on the passion in front of a crowd when he needed to, and he went on to give a dazzling speech setting out how the proposed canal would be ninety-three miles long with an additional twenty-six miles of branch lines to key towns like his home town of Leek as well as Derby. He detailed the locks the canal would need and how he would bore the two-mile long tunnel through Harecastle Hill. With conviction he assured the meeting that completion of the canal would require the construction of 127 aqueducts and culverts. Despite his reputation for not making formal plans Brindley was able to present a map of the proposed route and even recommended someone to print it in Manchester to Wedgwood. It was an impressive performance.

No doubt somewhat stupefied, the potential investors in the crowd asked him some questions. If they were to add their names to those of Gower, Bridgewater, Wedgwood (Josiah and John), Gilbert (Thomas and John) and Brindley himself, they needed some reassurance first. The most obvious question was cost. Brindley set out a budget of sorts that suggested the sum of £700 a mile to cover the cost of buying land and constructing locks, towpaths and bridges, £1,000 a mile for actually cutting the canal, and a nominal £10,000 for the two miles of tunnelling.

This added up to a total just over £150,000, which although a lot seems on reflection very reasonable, given that the Duke of Bridgewater calculated that he had spent much more than this on his own, somewhat shorter and lockless canal. It is doubtful whether anyone other than the Duke would have known this however, and even if the figure had been challenged, its supporters could have pointed to the considerable anticipated savings from giving the canal a narrow gauge.

An example of the confidence Brindley must have displayed that night can be seen in a report of a meeting with the canal's committee two years later when he declared he could build the canal in five years. This seemed improbable and when challenged he retorted with a wager of £200 that it would be done. As it turned out, in this respect at least, it was fortunate for Brindley that he was not to live another five years as he would have lost, and lost handsomely. Another example of his confidence was the fact that, in a statement of his growing wealth, he subscribed for thirty shares himself.

For many of those present at Wolseley Bridge the array of names before them must have been almost overwhelming. Despite his outwardly avuncular manner Josiah Wedgwood was well known to be an astute businessman who didn't suffer fools gladly. The Duke of Bridgewater was also an impressive figure. Although most had probably regarded him at some point as completely mad he had proved them all wrong. Earl Gower had shown himself to be a talented politician and that too took skill. As for this man Brindley, well he might look a bit ordinary, but no one had yet found a way of beating him in an argument about engineering.

The prospect of investing in something that might change the face of the nation must have been appealing. Probably more compelling though was the prospect of making a killing. Not surprisingly, the committee got its investors, subscribing a total of 505 shares of £200 each,

The bridge at Gailey Wharf has a separate aperture to take the horses that towed the boats down the canal.

The bridge at Fradley Junction, where the Staffordshire and Worcester Canal meets the Trent & Mersey Canal.

Gailey Wharf in Staffordshire sits on the summit of the Staffordshire & Worcester Canal and has an unusual circular toll-keepers tower, which made it easy to spot oncoming traffic from all directions.

making a total of just over £100,000 as initial working capital. A deal was also struck to buy off the turnpike lobby by offering to carry stone, gravel and other material for repairing roads for free. To placate the farming crowd they borrowed a trick out of the Duke of Bridgewater's book and offered to carry dung for free and to charge only half tolls for lime used as fertiliser.

Although at first there had been some discussion over whether to create a joint stock company (an alternative was a trust), once this was agreed the arrangements made were remarkably democratic, with no individual in the end allowed to own more than twenty shares. Two further subscriptions of £70,000 each in 1770 and 1775 were eventually required to finish the canal, but even with these the whole enterprise was delivered at a remarkably reasonable cost.

Early in 1766 Brindley once more found himself in London arguing the case for a canal. Although there was resistance from the navigation companies, Brindley and his committee got their way. On 14 May the Grand Trunk Canal received its Act of Parliament. Although significant, perhaps equally importantly the first branch off the proposed canal, that for the Staffordshire & Worcester Canal, also received its Act that day. This canal was more than just a spur, it provided a link to the Severn and thence to Bristol, thereby creating another of the arms of Brindley's Grand Cross.

This was symbolic, as this canal, running off a spur at Great Hayward just north of Shugborough Hall, home today to the Earl of Litchfield, would link both this canal and the Duke of Bridgewater's to the River Severn, passing through to the iron foundries of Coalbrookdale where Brindley had gone to get parts cast for his first steam engine. This idea killed off plans for a separate Severn to Mersey canal which, if it had gone ahead, would have been just as great an undertaking as the Trent & Mersey.

The Staffordshire & Worcester Canal is a classic Brindley achievement. It hugs contours and follows the valleys cut by natural rivers wherever practicable, in this case those of the Penk and Sow, followed by the Stour. In this way the need for locks was minimised, even if this was at the cost of longer overall length. Aqueducts were built over the Sow and the Trent as Brindley began to almost flaunt his new-found abilities. On reaching the Severn the canal was still twenty-nine feet above the river, but it was decided to build the basin at that height given the Severn's justified reputation for flooding. In time the basin, Stourport, was to become one of the most significant inland ports in the country.

The Staffordshire & Worcester was also where Brindley finally built his first lock, at Compton outside Wolverhampton at the southern end of the summit, in 1766. This followed experiments with the system in his garden at Turnhurst. The summit itself ends at Gailey Wharf, where a round tower was built for the toll collector's convenience.

Although work proceeded quickly, canals were still the object of suspicion for many, if nothing else an imposition on the natural landscape. A classic example of the need for Brindley and his followers to tread carefully with local landowners occurred at Tixall Wide. Here the local landowner, Thomas Clifford, had employed the ubiquitous Capability Brown to improve his gardens.

Brown loved lakes, but loathed canals. The result was a deal whereby Brindley got his canal through Clifford's land by broadening it into an ornamental lake, a result that went against the grain for him, being unnecessary additional work, but one that also demonstrates his pragmatism. Ironically only the gatehouse remains of the house but the lake is still there, a beautiful spot and a haunt of kingfishers.

The spine of the system however was to be the Grand Trunk. On 10 June 1766 a meeting was held at The Crown Inn at Stone that appointed Brindley as the Surveyor-General of the canal at a salary of £200 a year. Hugh Henshall, by now Brindley's brother-in-law, was made Clerk of Works at £150 a year and Josiah Wedgwood, astute businessman that he was, offered to be Treasurer at no salary. The Committee of Management also included such names as John Brindley, James' brother, and Matthew Boulton, later to partner James Watt in developing the commercial steam engine. To this day a sign on a bridge at Stone proclaims the town to be the birthplace of the Trent & Mersey Canal.

Perhaps, though, an equal claim to parentage can be filed by Burslem in the Potteries as six weeks later the first sod of earth was cut at Longbridge, which in time developed as the main wharfside for Burslem and came to be renamed Longport. This event was accompanied by some serious partying. Wedgwood did the honours, but others followed with their own symbolic plunges with a spade and the whole event was rounded off with a sheep roast in the town's market square, as well as a bonfire in the grounds of Wedgwood's house for more lowly guests.

Wedgwood must have been delighted. At last his long-cherished dream was becoming a reality, along with a means of securing the long-term viability of his beloved Potteries. In the same way that his pottery had chimed a chord with both royalty and the masses so the canal

As time went on, aqueducts became something of a signature feature of Brindley canals, such as this one at Haywood.

scheme he has a good claim to be the father of struck a chord with the times. Amongst the Georgian equivalent of the chattering classes, comprised almost entirely of men and meeting mainly in clubs, canals became a hot topic. They seemed to echo perfectly with the move towards more rational ways of doing things, as seen elsewhere in industrial processes and improved farming techniques. They also fitted well with the idea of man taking control of nature, in the belief and interest in the new sciences.

This was also a period of uncertainty, both socially and economically, and canals offered perhaps one means of addressing these issues. If, as they promised, they could even out some of the inequalities of distribution of wealth and resources that were a natural consequence of a poor national transport infrastructure then all to the good. It was difficult to argue against the prospect of cheap fuel and better supplies of food to the cities.

This was also the beginning of a period of economic slump, which in turn led to incidences of industrial unrest and even political agitation. In the countryside there was a series of poor harvests and rising prices and anything that might help ease the lot of the farmer was to be welcomed – hence the Duke of Bridgewater's repeated offers of free transport for manure.

At the same time, capital was plentiful and looking for a home at a time when interest rates were low at around three per cent. In time canals were to become the investment of choice of the 'middling sort', with stakes available in affordable £50 shares, an early forerunner of the wider share ownership precipitated by the privatisation of BT and other utilities around 200 years later. It probably also helped that investment income remained untaxed through this period, taxes being mainly levied on consumption, something a vibrant economy helped to perpetuate.

There was also encouragement from the state, which recognised the potential power of canals to encourage trade, something it welcomed in order to up the tempo of an economy it

This modest signpost at Great Haywood speaks the truth, but belies the significance of this point on the inland waterways system.

was increasingly keen to tax. After the parliamentary battle for permission to build the Grand Trunk canal acts faced little opposition from decision makers in London. Parliamentary time had become increasingly devoted to private bills around this period, with Government seeing its role less as the initiator of policy than the arbiter of initiatives from individuals or private companies. Not that all private acts were state-improving however, divorce still required an Act of Parliament for example.

Most of all, canals hit the mood by offering an alternative to the misery that was the road system. Despite the fact that turnpikes were becoming more and more established, to the point that they had spread to offer a cobweb of communications across the country, they still had serious limitations. The Grand Cross in particular offered the prospect of a co-ordinated set of super-highways in a system previously dominated by muddy tracks. They were an idea whose time had come.

Not that everything in the canal camp was rosy. As with the Bridgewater, opposition existed to the very concept of canals and arguments were constructed against them wherever possible. Innkeepers would go bankrupt they argued. The breed of English horses would be destroyed. Even the old saw that the jolly jack tar who manned the navy would disappear reappeared. Generally, this group were simply against change, always a powerful lobby, and they received an audience. Although today change has become a way of life, in pre-industrial times it was something to be seen as threatening and unwelcome, especially after what seemed to have been a long period of relative stability. Change was for some too closely allied to chaos.

Although Brindley was probably subconsciously aware of these moods it is less likely that they acted as his main motivator. Having shown the way with the Bridgewater it is highly possible that Brindley, ever the improver, wanted a chance to modify and better his techniques, and what could be better than a scheme that transcended all that had gone before it. Brindley was rarely troubled by the size of a challenge, being more intrigued by its nature. Part of the attraction of building the Grand Trunk would have been the numerous challenges not yet even envisaged. Like many engineers after him, for Brindley the whole thing was technically feasible so why not have a go at doing it?

On a more personal level he may also have seen the Grand Trunk as unfinished business. He had been involved with the scheme before the Bridgewater Canal had captured his every waking hour and might have seen it as an unresolved problem, requiring his unique brand of thinking. Once others started to get involved so Brindley seemed to be goaded on to ensure that the proposed solution was 'right', by which he of course meant his solution. He may also have had some sense of destiny, both that it was his fate to make this canal happen and that this was a way of securing his place in history.

Already by this time Brindley was a less than well man, complaining more and more of aches and pains and finding the whole business of life increasingly tiring. By now he was in his fifties and by Georgian standards no spring chicken. Certainly a life lived on the road, eating at inns and sleeping in strange beds, to say nothing of the constant stress he was under, was hardly conducive to good health, no matter how much compensation married life was giving him.

Despite this he started work pretty much straight away on what everyone knew was going to be the trickiest part of the route, the tunnel through Harecastle at the canal's summit. The decision to bore a tunnel, the first in the country to be started for purely transport purposes (others finished before it), must have been a difficult one; but when all options had been

As well as being one of the oldest pubs on the waterways, the Star Inn at Stone is also one of the most unusual.

considered there really was little realistic alternative. Indeed, as the Grand Trunk grew, tunnels became something of a signature feature, with the completed canal having five in total with a combined length of a little under three miles, more than half of which was represented by the Harecastle.

The proposed undertaking at Harecastle was huge and it didn't take long for Brindley's critics to re-emerge from the woodwork with more 'castles in the air' type jibes, despite the fact that the Barton Aqueduct continued to be a resounding success. Not least amongst these were those who stood to lose out if the canal turned out to be successful, including those whose objections had been rejected by Parliament.

It is easy to see why they saw it as Brindley's potential nemesis. Tunnelling was a hugely unpredictable activity fraught with danger. No one really knew what they were going to encounter until picks struck rock. Understanding of basic geology at this time was weak and hills such as Harecastle yielded their innermost secrets only with some reluctance.

As we know, Brindley had some more than nominal experience of tunnel construction, notably the work he had undertaken at the Wet Earth Colliery, but even he would, quite literally, be pitching in the dark. Not surprisingly he recruited from those with day-to-day experience of working their way through rock: miners, a good proportion of whom were of hardy Irish stock. Technically, at least according to Brindley, it looked possible. The question his detractors were posing was, was it really necessary?

True to type, wherever possible on this canal Brindley would twist and turn his route, hugging the contour as if for warmth in an effort to keep the water flat and manageable and most of all to avoid any need for locks or tunnels. With the Trent and Mersey we can see the full extent of his aversion to locks by the enthusiasm with which he promoted tunnelling as an alternative. To the north of Harecastle he wound the water so that it was possible to navigate all the way from Middlewich in Cheshire to Manchester without having to lock once – although today a single short-drop stop lock separates this canal from the Bridgewater.

Harecastle Hill at Tunstall just outside Stoke on Trent represented a formidable obstacle. At 100 feet high a cutting wasn't practical and locking wasn't really an option because its location coincided with the summit of the canal. If locks were cut into the hill it would have been impossible to supply them without resort to serious pumping. One plus point was the fact that the hill contained coal, so the lesson of Worsley, that mines could provide both profit and, just as essentially water, was well understood and took some of the pain away from the decision.

By boring through the hill he would be able to quite literally tap into most of the water he needed. Like the Bridgewater, the canal would be able to operate totally independently from the surrounding rivers and their often rapacious owners. As he probably anticipated, the water would be a thundering nuisance while the tunnel was being bored, but this would be a temporary inconvenience to be balanced with the benefit it would deliver over time.

It is worth noting that the Golden Hill Colliery, which worked the Harecastle coal, was part owned by Brindley and John Gilbert. When the tunnel was complete a network of minor tunnels linked it to the coal seams, thus allowing for coal to be loaded straight onto boats and avoiding having to cart it out and round the hill. Charitably we have to assume that this had no influence upon the decision to tunnel in the first place.

In Brindley's defence, when the great engineer Thomas Telford was commissioned to build another tunnel fifty years later he chose the same route. Also, although this may be less of a vindication, British Rail chose to go through the hill when faced with the same set of choices. The sheer technical elegance of this solution would have appealed to Brindley, as would the challenge. He knew that the tunnel would dictate the time it would take to complete the canal, but he stuck to his five-year prediction.

The decision to bore into Harecastle also solved another problem – the width of the canal. To save costs it was agreed to halve the proposed width of the tunnel in order to save on digging and therefore costs. Brindley even decided to do without a towpath, a decision no doubt rued by subsequent boatmen who had to 'leg' their way through the tunnel. This decision essentially set a new narrow gauge for canals and helped to inform the standard dimensions of locks. It also meant that a whole new type of boat had to be developed, the narrow boat that is today synonymous with the inland waterways. Previously, the Bridgewater had used a variant of riverboats.

In the interim, work started on other sections of the canal and, within a year, ten miles had been completed. It might have been more. In the first report to the Management Committee it was noted that '… more might have been done but the attention of the company has been chiefly employed in the most difficult part of the work … the principal of these is the great hill called Harecastle through which a tunnel is making, of an oval form, in height twelve feet and in breadth eight feet ten inches'. By way of mitigation the same report marvelled that 'For half a mile on each side of this hill the canal is of an extraordinary dimension, which will be the reservoir for the water which flows out of the hill both ways in great abundance'. It was also noted that one lock had been completed and 'some others [are] in great forwardness'. Four road bridges had also been built and 'materials prepared for many more'.

Within two years twenty-two miles had been cut, more than the length of the Bridgewater and within four years it was possible to travel from Great Haywood and the junction with the Staffs and Worcester, also under construction at the time, and Weston-on-Trent, east of Burton. Already fourteen locks had been completed, twenty-six road bridges and even six boats. The following year the first section on the upward run towards the Mersey was opened to Stone. For the shareholders this progress was a cause for celebration. So long as Mr Brindley delivered his tunnel, they were going to get their canal. Once again the good people of Staffordshire showed their enthusiasm for a party, going so far as to employ a cannon for effect, the firing of which unfortunately took out a newly built bridge and lock.

Josiah Wedgwood set the tone for this confidence. Even before the first stretch of the canal had opened he had gone into partnership with his old friend John Bentley and opened a new factory on a green field site by the banks of the proposed canal. With typical panache and foresight he created a model village for his workers to live alongside the factory and named the whole area Etruria, after that part of Italy north of the Tiber known for its Etruscan pottery. Apparently feeling no awkwardness he also constructed a mansion for himself, which he named Etruria Hall, opposite the factory and looking down on the site of the canal and village.

Equally significantly, it was around this time that both the Coventry and Oxford canals were being proposed, with Brindley being actively involved in a viability survey. The former would link with the Trent and Mersey at Fradley and join up with the latter at Braunston in Northamptonshire. Critically, from Brindley's point of view, together these canals would provide a link south to the Thames, thus completing his vision of a Grand Cross linking the four main seaports of England.

Today's Harecastle Tunnel Belongs to Thomas Telford, although Brindley's original is still visible to the right.

A meeting at the Three Tuns in Banbury on the 25 October 1768 was held 'to receive Mr Brindley's report and to take the proposal into full consideration'. The Coventry stretch was estimated at £50,000, which was instantly subscribed at the meeting through 500 shares of £100 each paying five per cent interest a year.

Meanwhile Mr Brindley was indeed making progress, but not as fast as he had planned. At a General Meeting of the Canal Company held on 1 October 1768, two years into construction, it was noted that 409 yards had been completed, less than a fifth of the total. As he was no doubt at pains to explain however, this represented more than a fifth of the work. Before a single yard could be cut Brindley had had to sink a number of shafts down from the top of the hill, with a face opened out on opposite ends at their base.

Surveying techniques were crude, with the shafts put into some kind of rough alignment. Surveying still being in its infancy this often involved the use of a telescope to line up markers across the top of the hill. As such, it is hardly surprising that most canal tunnels possess a dogleg or two as they wend their path through. Depths were gauged using a plumb line and the rock was hacked out using the same basic picks that had created the mine entrance at Worsley. The shafts ranged from 210 to 240 feet deep and there were fifteen of them. With digging also taking place at either portal, this meant that in total the hill was being attacked on thirty-two fronts, a logistical nightmare.

What was more, nature and the hill fought back. Brindley had no choice but to try to maintain a single level, regardless of the rock formation. Needless to say, this was not uniform in rock type and the miners were confronted by, in turns, millstone grit, ironstone and, according

Stone is demonstrably proud of its claim to be the birthplace of the Trent & Mersey Canal, as shown by the sign over a bridge entering the town.

to some of the contractors involved, some of the hardest rock they had ever encountered, followed by soft sand and coal. Most of all there was the predicted water, and lots of it.

It soon became clear that Brindley's unique skills with water would need to be drawn on and many of the expedients that had proved their worth at Worsley and elsewhere were brought into action again. Steam engines were erected to pump out water supplementing the efforts of cruder pumps powered by the wind, men or horses. At the same time to counter the effects of a build up of dangerous gases, Brindley again used his tried and tested technique of underground fires to force updraughts that carried the gases away.

From a distance the hill must have seemed almost alive, with pockets of activity and noise linked by men and horses trawling muddy tracks between them. The hissing of crude steam engines would have competed with the clank of picks on rock and the slosh of water and mud. Ripe language would have echoed up from underground in a mixture of dialects, counterpointed by complaining squeaks from overloaded wheelbarrows on the surface.

Every day would have brought fresh challenges and the wretched individuals whose job it was to cope with them would most probably have laughed at the hyperbole directed at Brindley by a contemporary who suggested that 'he handles rocks as easily as you would plum-pies and makes the four elements subservient to his will'. The same commentator, however, also suggested that what he had witnessed was 'the eighth wonder of the world', summing up the feeling of many outside observers at the time. Whether participant or spectator, it was clear that something significant was going on.

Workings from the digging were hauled up by ropes and dragged away by horse and cart. Pure muscle power, co-ordinated by ingenuity, was conquering nature, but slowly. Although he supervised the works at Harecastle and elsewhere along the canal, Brindley was also in demand from the growing schools of entrepreneurs and speculators looking to cut their own canals. Feverishly Brindley obliged their needs, driven perhaps in part by a desire to see his visions fulfilled, and in part by the sheer excitement and challenge of it all, and much of his time was spent on horseback ferrying between different locations. Not many men get the chance to scrawl their signature across the landscape of their country and it wasn't an opportunity Brindley was going to pass up.

As the tunnel bored a passage through the hillside it was arched and lined with brick. Inch by sweaty inch the passage progressed. Around 600 miners were involved in the digging, supported by a small army of horses and hauliers on the surface. The technical achievement of what they were undertaking is hard now to comprehend, especially as, like Barton, it had never been done before. The engineering of the Harecastle Tunnel, however, made the Barton Aqueduct look like a student project, being both bigger and bolder in concept and execution. Even so, it was still largely a case of ropes, picks and barrows multiplied by men and divided by the inspiration that made it happen.

In the end it took eleven years to complete, and although Brindley was not to survive that long it remains probably his greatest achievement. Like the M25 motorway, it was so successful that the traffic using it demanded extra capacity and fifty years later Thomas Telford would be commissioned to build a replacement. Techniques had moved on sufficiently in the interim for this tunnel to be completed in only three years, and although superior in engineering terms it was still only as wide as a single boat and for years it ran in parallel with Brindley's masterpiece, traffic going north taking the new tunnel, that going south the old.

It was the local coal works that ultimately did for the tunnel. Unwittingly Brindley's own colliery contributed to the subsidence that caused it to sink slowly over the years. Today it looks barely high enough to take a dog on a surfboard, the entrance slumped down like an old man's shoulders. Modern photographs of the inside suggest a gaping shark's jaw and throat, with stalactites representing dripping saliva.

The canal was about more than the tunnel however. Equally impressive was the flight of over thirty locks south of Middlewich that hauled the canal up towards its summit, known both then and today quite legitimately as 'Heartbreak Hill', with eight or nine foot deep cavernous single locks that scream out as they empty. There were also more aqueducts, over a 150 of them, and 100 plus road bridges.

In digging the canal the navvies were reminded daily of the reasons why they were bothering. A whole range of different materials revealed themselves from just below the surface, many of which had a value if only they could be transported to where they might be wanted. The country's natural wealth was being exposed and among the materials found was salt in Cheshire, the presence of which had been known and exploited since Roman times.

Less well known were different types of stone, including limestone at Burton, coal, iron ore and marl. Each had its use and encouraged different industries from mining to construction, from ironworks to agriculture. Clay excavated from the Harecastle tunnel was used to bake bricks for the bridges. The canal rapidly became more than a simple highway, acting as a catalyst for a whole new layer of local industry, which in turn required services and spawned support activity. Inland ports developed at convenient points or junctions. Ale houses and supply points sprung up along the route. Not only did the potters of Staffordshire benefit, but whole swathes of the country, previously barely inhabited, underwent the equivalent of a Georgian regeneration programme.

This was a seminal moment in the development of the country. The sheer physical presence of the canals across the previously under-utilised fields of England emphasised that industry now took precedence over agriculture. Resources had become mobile, and along with them people and ideas. As with the Internet in our own time, markets became more perfect, knowledge more widespread.

Limits on human ambition were lifted. From simply accepting your lot it became okay to strive for more. This attitude was summed up by the economist Adam Smith who declared that it was 'the right of every man to better his condition'. The puritans were dead and buried. The wheels of capitalism had found their grease, from this point on it was every man for himself.

As Brindley had expected, when the tunnel at Harecastle was opened in 1777 it marked the completion of the canal. In the end the canal had taken eleven years and £296,000 to finish – nearly half as much again as he had suggested, but he never was a great estimator. As with Barton, the tunnel became a tourist attraction and from this point on there could be no doubt as to Brindley's position in canal history.

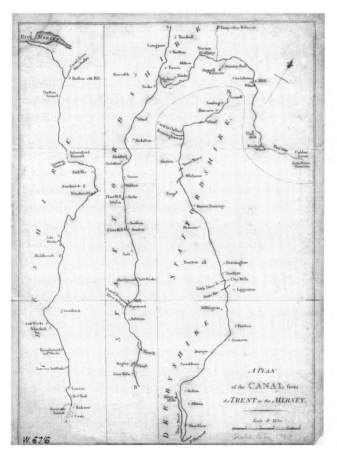

This map of the Trent and Mersey Canal shows clearly how Brindley saw the route as his 'Grand Trunk', the artery that would form the basis of his plan to link the country's four main seaports through a network of inland waterways. (Courtesy of The Waterways Archive)

nine

James Brindley –
Canal Engineer

It is often said of James Brindley that his most appropriate memorial is the canal system itself, the vast majority of which survives to this day. It is true that there is an occasional flare up of interest in him, leading perhaps to a fresh statue or the naming of a building or street after him, yet despite this attention he has never quite made the leap from canal-cult hero to recognition amongst a wider audience.

In a 2001 BBC poll of the greatest Britons of all time Brindley failed to register at all, his claims superseded by those of the likes of Dame Julie Andrews and Johnny Rotten. This irony is compounded when one reflects that the runner up in the poll, second only to Winston Churchill, was Brunel, the engineer who was to the railways what Brindley was to the canals. It seems that the canals are doomed always to play second fiddle to the railways.

One spate of interest occurred in the mid-1950s, when Brindley's birthplace and grave were spruced up and given shiny new metal plaques. The one currently bolted to his grave is plain and bold. The words on it describe him simply as a 'Canal Engineer', making no claim to pre-eminence, and gives a brief list of his life's main points. Although factually accurate, this representation of his life reveals little of the personality of the man buried beneath, but it is perhaps appropriate. Brindley was a plain, modest man who would have wanted to be remembered for his achievements rather than his character.

Stretching the analogy further, the grave's position is also perhaps symbolic. Although towards the front of the graveyard, it is shunted to one side, having been moved from its original, more prominent position next to the church many years ago. There is no railing round it and no headstone. A vigorous rhododendron bush periodically hides the grave from view. You have to ask a local resident where it is because there is nothing to tell you how to find it.

In a similar way, in the years immediately after his death Brindley's reputation continued to bask in brilliance, but the passage of time has inexorably caused it to become overshadowed. Occasionally, the determined efforts of supporters prune back some of the obfuscation and let the light shine in once more, but their efforts are only temporarily effective as what seems to be the natural order always seems to reassert itself.

To test the case for a further pruning, and by implication any claims to greatness, it is perhaps best to start with an appreciation of the man and what seemed to make him tick. In a world defined by images it is natural to start by studying the scarce portraits of him that survive. One of these, a miniature still owned by his family, reproduced on page 19 shows him face on, a slightly shy smile directed at the portraitist shining out from a ruddy well-fleshed face, the most distinguishing feature of which is the deep-set eyes. The face is framed by a fancy but not ostentatious curled wig and a white cravat beneath, supporting what is a definite double chin. Below is a well-cut snuff coat and waistcoat. This is, every inch, the image of a successful man.

Another picture (see page 56), showing him in half profile and three-quarter-length coat, shows him in similar attire and reveals a slight stomach. In this, the cravat is peeking out from one of the brass buttons on his long waistcoat as if he had absent-mindedly forgotten to tuck it in. One of his white-cuffed hands rests on a brass theodolite, half of which he folds under his arm like a gentleman's shotgun. This is very possibly the self-same instrument that survives today on display at the Brindley Mill in Leek, although pedants might just point out that this is actually a level as it registers only in the horizontal not the vertical as well.

Both of these portraits would have been painted towards the end of Brindley's career, during his heyday as the undisputed leader of the canal pack, and one of them only survives because his widow asked Josiah Wedgwood to retrieve it from the artist. Brindley, it seems, had sent him away with a flea in his ear after he had taken offence at the manner in which the artist had asked for payment.

As we have seen, it took Brindley some years to achieve the pre-eminence required to be the subject of a portrait and during those years he had to undergo significant privation and struggle. Only when his success was beyond doubt did he succumb to its trappings. Brindley's story is not one of a man unrecognised in his lifetime. In his final years he lived well, enjoyed social prestige and even commissioned his own coat of arms. The tragedy is that those years were so few, leaving too little time for him to consolidate his reputation and thereby cement his place in history, something it has been left for a succession of guardians to do after the event, and not that successfully. Brindley tried his best, by playing the card that many subsequent icons have found successful, that of dying young, but in his case it worked against him.

Although it might be perfectly reasonable for someone who had achieved as much as he had to be concerned about how he might be remembered, we have no evidence that this was something that ever occupied James Brindley. Throughout his life he was a man who let his achievements do the talking. He had neither the education, time nor inclination to be a self-publicist. Perhaps if he had had more of the blood and bluster of Brunel he too might have a higher place in the consciousness of today's public.

This is not to belittle his understanding of the need to cultivate good public relations, which he exercised to the benefit of canals in general rather than for his own benefit. Having observed a master at work, namely Francis Egerton, later in his career Brindley would be highly conscious of the need to cultivate good relations with the owners of the land his canals went through. If a fence got damaged in the course of building a canal he would ensure it was replaced rather than simply repaired. On a higher level he also understood the need to place canals in a positive light with potential subscribers to new schemes and decision makers in Parliament. The whole idea of artificial inland waterways was not yet fixed in the public psyche and their benefits needed to be sold constantly.

These arguments were fought on practicalities not personalities, and probably just as well. Brindley was almost certainly a hard man to warm to. His frequent certainty that he was right must have come across as arrogance, his need to retreat from debate and dialogue, so that he could be sure that he was right, as aloofness. His behaviour shows all the hallmarks of an intuitive introvert. He would observe, make connections, analyse and see patterns before putting forward his conclusions, but would prefer to do all this alone, relying on his inner resources to reach those conclusions rather than sharing mindwork in progress with others. Brindley was perhaps fortunate in the masters that fate dealt him, in that they indulged him in his habits, but it was usually a mutually beneficial relationship.

This natural preference was simply part of his personality, but has been interpreted by some to suggest that he was not a good verbal communicator. The evidence suggests otherwise. Not only did he prove to be a persuasive speaker on a number of important occasions, ranging from a Parliamentary Committee through to public subscription meetings for new canals, but a poor verbal communicator would not have been able to convince his paymasters of the validity of his often outlandish ideas, or to explain to simple labourers what it was he wanted done.

Like many introverts, Brindley could be eloquent if boosted by the self-confidence born of being on his subject. He could even act the showman, as his proffered bet on the completion of the Trent and Mersey and performances with chalk and cheese before Parliament demonstrate. Furthermore, he knew enough about being a showman to appreciate the need to look the part. If this meant spending freely on the necessary clothes, then this was what he did, even if the amounts incurred were sufficiently significant to be recorded item by item in his journal.

Rather, what Brindley did not seem to appreciate were challenges to his ideas. The greatest clash of personalities in his career was probably that with John Gilbert, a man who was in many ways his equal, at least in terms of status, during the building of the Bridgewater Canal. The contretemps between these two were legendary, but usually occurred when one invaded the perceived territory of the other. In other words their differences tended to be professional rather than personal. Indeed the pair went on to enjoy a number of successful business relationships to their mutual advantage.

It is also often suggested that Brindley was not a natural written communicator, with many commentators suggesting that he could barely write. Although the idea of an illiterate man from humble beginnings rising to fame and fortune, the classic tale of rags to riches, might have appealed to the romanticism of Victorian biographers, the evidence again suggests otherwise.

The lead exhibit in this evidence is Brindley's journals, which have been quoted frequently in the telling of this story. Although these are not comprehensive, they do provide a valuable first-hand record for many of the crucial years of Brindley's career, critically *in his own hand*. Hard-covered notebooks of plain paper, no more than three inches by five, these comprise a combination of diary, expense record, memory jogger and spare paper for the odd calculation. At times they are methodical, at other times random. What they are not is the work of an illiterate man.

Brindley was diligent in recording his time and financial details, showing an attention to detail befitting an engineer. The hand is florid but perfectly readable. Columns of dates often run down the side of the page recording where he worked that day and what he did. It is true that the spelling and grammar are inconsistent and often jarring to the modern eye. The

Botterham on the Staffordshire & Worcester Canal in a scene probably taken around the 1910. (Courtesy of The Waterways Archive)

word 'engine' is, for example, variously spelt 'engon' or 'engin'. This needs to be considered in the context of its day however. Dr Johnson had only published his famous dictionary offering standard spellings for common words in 1755 and at this time phonetic use of language was still considered perfectly normal. Even the word 'canal' was often spelt as 'canel' by Brindley and others, it is even spelt this way on Hugh Henshall's gravestone.

The journals also betray the personality of someone cute with money, with the author recording every last penny spent in the pursuit of his business in order to make sure that wherever possible these were recharged to his clients. A common record was the amount of money 'in my pokit (pocket)' at the beginning of any fresh journey. Again, columns of figures are annotated in the journals, along with additions and subtractions, which are never wrong.

It is true that none of Brindley's plans survive, fuelling the rumour, and again the Victorian fancy, that he never produced them, either because he couldn't or because he retained all the information he needed in his head. Although it is possible to accept he may have made his critical calculations in his head, in his journals and elsewhere references are made to plans, so it would seem that he could, and if necessary did, produce them.

His brother-in-law and later biographer Hugh Henshall claimed that Brindley would only record figures at critical stages of a problem, not the workings behind them, a habit that more precise colleagues must have found infuriating, especially when he was invariably proved to be right. On the larger schemes he was involved in it is difficult to see how he could have delegated the work required without some kind of written instruction, especially given his frequent absences from the site. This quirk may again be put down to personal preference. As his performances before Parliament showed, he preferred practical demonstrations to written ideas.

The journals are also interesting for the light they shed on his personal habits, not least the minutiae of how he lived his life in the rare moments when he wasn't working. Meticulously, Brindley would record the inns that were his home when he was on the road, including what he ate. A constant diet of beer and pub food did nothing for his waistline, despite the regular exercise he got through riding his horse and dashing around all points of the compass. Again however, there was not the paranoia for thinness that exists today, and an expanding midriff was, if anything, a sign of his growing success. One story goes that he enjoyed his food so much that he would eat until his stomach hoisted a designated button on his waistcoat to a specific place, at which point he would stop – a very precise engineer's solution.

Brindley revisionists have suggested that he was also a drinker, fond of taking a swig from his 'pocket pistol' or hipflask of spirits that he kept constantly in his waistcoat. The originator of this theory was Francis Egerton – not the one who financed the Bridgewater Canal but the eighth Duke, some years after Brindley's death. Apparently enraged by a belief that his esteemed ancestor's reputation had become overshadowed by his engineer's, he penned a hatchet job in 1820 in which he claimed that far from being the mastermind behind the Barton Aqueduct Brindley 'ran away from it, to Stretford, and never appeared again until the bridge became secure'.

Referring to Brindley's supposed drink problem he contrasted his behaviour later in life to when he had first entered the Duke's service when he claimed that Brindley would regularly 'drink a basin of milk in the morning before he went among the workmen'. In this case it is tempting to cast Brindley as the victim of a cocktail of some severely sour grapes and early nineteenth-century mores. Again, it is also important to place these reports in the context of Brindley's time, when a swift dram or two during the day would not have been seen as anything exceptional.

A stronger theme emerging from the journals, and comments made about him at the time, was Brindley's sheer relentless energy and passion for his work. He was a practical man, impatient to see his ideas proven and put into action, even if it meant getting his own hands dirty. Anecdotes about him tossing his papers to one side and jumping into ditches to show how something should be done, or metaphorically putting his own shoulder to a stuck wheel, abound.

However, although Brindley could just about cope with the implementation of smaller scale projects such as mills, larger scale project management was not his strength. Even one of his best friends, Erasmus Darwin, was moved to observe that 'he was better qualified to be the contriver than the manager of a great design'. Furthermore, despite his facility with numbers, he was not a good estimator of costs, as the Duke of Bridgewater was the first to discover. This may also go some way to explain why he took so long to establish his own business in Leek. Although it probably came as cold comfort, the financiers of all the canals Brindley had an early hand in would discover that his enthusiasm for the project in hand blinded him to the finance required.

Until his final few years, when he discovered the joys of marriage and family, Brindley's work was his life. He seemed to enjoy few outside pursuits and even when relaxing would prefer to talk about a work problem than put the world to rights. His visit to see Garrick perform Richard III and the apparent brainstorm that followed offers a good example of this. Another story suggests that as his fame spread he turned down an invitation from the King of

France to visit the Grand Canal of Languedoc on the basis that there was little value in simply seeing the canal if he wasn't being asked to improve it.

Again, this approach could be put down to a seam of arrogance manifesting at times as sulkiness. A charitable view would suggest obstinacy; a critical one though would charge him with bloody-mindedness. An illustration of this would be his approach to toothache, a common complaint at the time. Showing a touching faith in the power of water, the element that defined his life, he would alternately pour very cold and then very hot water on an infected area as a sort of punishment for the pain, claiming that 'if it spites me, I will spite it', whether or not the cure worked.

The fact is that Brindley was not a culturally sophisticated man. Like a true introvert he was comfortable in the company of men such as Darwin and Wedgwood on a one to one basis, but never really embraced the opportunity to enter their intellectual circles. He was a product of his background and his special capacity with water. His childhood had taken place against a background of relative poverty followed by relative comfort. During the period his parents were ostracised from the rest of his father's family life was undoubtedly hard, but after they had been welcomed back to the bosom of that family their circumstances would have compared well with the average rural household.

Whilst, in time, Brindley enjoyed the trappings of wealth, he remained true to his background and never pretended to be something he wasn't. If this meant that at times he came across as sulky or a rough diamond, then that was just the way he was. The Quaker's instinct was to be comfortable with their own company, and although not himself a Quaker, the influences of his childhood must have left a mark. Bloody-mindedness could equally be interpreted as single-mindedness, a quality his ancestors had held in spades. Furthermore, throughout his life Brindley exhibited a clear sense of right and wrong. When Bennett, his first master, fell on hard times Brindley supported him and his family despite the diabolical treatment he had received when first apprenticed to the man.

More critically, Brindley was also free with his knowledge. Perhaps subconsciously aware that he was living on borrowed time, he gathered around him a group of like-minded acolytes, a succeeding generation, to whom he passed on his theories and tricks of the trade. He became a good selector of men and a good delegator.

As a result, when he died the momentum towards canals did not die with him, sufficient intellectual property had been freely given to allow that next generation to pick up on his ideas and ideals. Former assistants who went on to greater things included Robert Whitworth, who worked on the Birmingham, Oxford and Coventry canals, Samuel Simcock, with whom he worked on the Staffordshire & Worcester, and Samuel Weston who constructed the Chester Canal and worked on the Oxford.

The image that emerges then is of a plainly dressed, plainly spoken, rather modest man with hidden depths and a talent for all things connected with water. When exercising this talent he could be opinionated but with justification, for he was usually right. When it came to dealing with water he had a unique ability to see things in the round. Like a good chess player he could see the potential impact on the outcome of a game flowing from a single move. His skills were intuitive, he could arrive at solutions that had baffled his peers through a process of observation and contemplation, and often these solutions were daring and brave, but also elegant and difficult to fault in terms of logic.

It is this dichotomy, between the plain façade and the inspirational mind, which attracted or repelled his peers. For men like Josiah Wedgwood and Francis Egerton, both of whom had undergone unusual upbringings themselves, Brindley was a refreshing phenomenon. For others, more steeped in a supposed natural hierarchy, he represented a challenge, or even worse than that, a threat.

A considerable section of society regarded canals as something of little or no interest to them, linked as they were to trade and parts of the country they never expected to visit. Nevertheless, he was indispensable. When the nagging of the committee behind the Oxford Canal became too much, Brindley felt no compunction in offering his resignation, causing the committee, consisting mainly of learned Oxford dons, to write a grovelling letter offering 'their very humble apologies if they have offended him'.

Brindley himself seemed untroubled by this divergence of opinion, preferring instead to concentrate on his work. As if to defy the image of a bluff millwright-made-good, on the quiet Brindley turned out to be rather an astute businessman. He took stakes in many of the canals he worked on, including £4,000 in the Trent and Mersey and £3,000 in the Oxford, and his share of the Golden Hill Colliery turned out to be a very wise investment. He also invested in his brother John's pottery and his purchase of Turnhurst Hall towards the end of his life would have been a clear statement of his success.

Indeed, Brindley's climb up the social ladder was a good example of what was possible within England's relatively fluid society at that time, relative, that is, to the rest of Europe where an aristocrat such as the Duke of Bridgewater would never have dreamed of such a visible move into 'trade'. Brindley's rise showed what was possible through industry and inventiveness, and he was not alone. Soon the country would have numerous examples of men who had 'made good', whose skill in making money would fuel the country's future economic dominance. Unlike in the rest of Europe, station was not predetermined by blood, a 'can do' spirit could be exercised, and Brindley was a prime example of this.

* * * * * * * * * *

Accounts of Brindley's life around the time of his death tended towards the hagiographic. Words like 'genius' were used freely and records of his life often read like a bid for beatification. Josiah Wedgwood led the way, writing to his partner Thomas Bentley shortly before Brindley's death that he feared his passing would rob the world of 'one of the great geniuses who seldom live to see justice done to their singular abilities'.

Wedgwood went on to suggest that the likes of Brindley 'must trust to future ages for that tribute of praise and fair fame they so greatly merit from their fellow mortals'. Within a generation, however, opinion was more divided. Egged on in part by the sour grapes of the then Francis Egerton, the revisionists started to rein back on some of the claims made for Brindley, not always without justification.

For others, however, the rags to riches story was irresistible, with one such example appearing in an 1834 book of 'memoirs of illustrious and eminent personages' by an unnamed author, which suggested that Brindley was 'A man who laboured under such great and numerous disadvantages as nothing but his ingenuity, perseverance and moral courage, could have surmounted; and yet, who, in spite of them all, attained a pre-eminence in his profession, which made him one of the great wonders, and one of the most important benefactors, of the age in which he appeared'.

The seminal summary of his life was probably that of Samuel Smiles, published in 1874 as part of a series on 'Great Engineers'. A journalist at heart, Smiles' account is flowery at times but detailed, preferring to avoid controversy if it got in the way of a good anecdote. Smiles had the advantage of access to sources now lost to the modern biographer and much of his account needs to be taken on trust. His romanticism seems to have set the tone for subsequent accounts that have focused on specific aspects of his life, such as his engineering achievements or his ancestry, usually in glowing terms. The central debate on the extent of Brindley's greatness therefore remains unresolved.

That Brindley was the first real canal engineer isn't open to question, but was he a genius? That claims to these titles can be made at all is probably justified by the fact that he was recognised as something special and unique even in his own lifetime, most notably by men history has subsequently recognised as great in their own right, such as Wedgwood. In addition, even after his death his standards remained the benchmark his successors aspired to match.

To start with basics, Brindley will justly be remembered for his discovery of the art of 'puddling' – the mixing together of sand and clay to make a watertight lining for artificial waterways. With this simple expedient he made it possible to create canals that didn't leak. Like all great discoveries it was simple but effective. It is also directly linked to his other great attribute, his affinity with water. He seemed to know instinctively how to tame and master nature's most fundamental element. This understanding led him to state that inland waterways should be a system to themselves, independent of the vagaries of nature such as flooding, drought and silt that would surely follow if they depended upon rivers. This went completely counter to the prevailing orthodoxy both in terms of science and what would have been regarded as natural common sense. Instead, Brindley took the best from nature, the valleys carved by rivers over time, and mastered it to his and his masters' benefit.

Brindley could sit and stare at a water system and get into its spirit, understanding how it flowed and where its strengths and weaknesses lay. It was said of him that he could estimate the fall of a brook simply by looking at it. Water which ran downhill he compared to a furious giant running along and overturning everything with a destructive force, whereas 'if you lay the giant flat upon his back he loses all his force and becomes completely passive, whatever his size might be'. The response was obvious: keep the water flat wherever you can and you can be its master. Before Brindley men had sought to work with water, after him they knew how to tame it.

This understanding led to many of the hallmarks of a Brindley canal: the hugging of a contour to preserve a stable level and his aversion to locks. Brindley liked his flat water in the same way that the Romans liked their straight roads, and each remain hallmarks of their style to this day. Perhaps the most overt example of this lies in the northern reaches of the Oxford Canal, which in its original, Brindley-esque incarnation would wander around like a drunken man, doubling back on itself in great loops in order to dodge the large number of streams in the canal's path and to stay at the same height. In the 1830s this led to a series of 'straightenings' that lopped a whole four miles off the original thirty-six-mile stretch between Coventry and the junction at Braunston.

Clearly at times some kind of device to negotiate a gradient is required – not even Brindley could always tunnel himself out of trouble – and locks were the answer. Although some enthusiasts are happy to give Brindley the credit for inventing these the idea of locks had been around since Anglo-Saxon times. Examples of pound locks, with a single gate at the top and a double gate at the bottom, can be found as far back as 1564 when they were used on the Exeter Ship Canal. As we have seen, Brindley's first locks were constructed on the Staffordshire & Worcester Canal in 1766 and at a meeting of the canal companies three years later in Litchfield a standard dimension of seventy-four feet nine inches long and seven feet wide was agreed. This standard also effectively endorsed Brindley's personal preference for 'narrow' canals, which he insisted caused less seepage, something else that stamped his mark upon history.

Brindley also developed the art of surveying topography and water to define the path a canal should take. Art rather than science because it was a combination of what he called 'reconnoitring' (both by eye and using his level) and intuition. Surveys remained imprecise for some time, with opinion on the best route a canal should take driven by vested interests as much as geography. The purpose of a survey was to define a possible route that could then be offered to Parliament for approval, and even then engineers had latitude to alter a course should circumstances dictate. Understanding of geology was crude, and navvies would often find themselves having to cope with unforeseen shifts in rock types as their digging progressed.

This effective rotating metal guard would have saved the bridge's side from exessive rope wear when horses were the main means of propulsion.

Having the skills, intuition, experience and at times just sheer nerve to deal with problems as they arose was another feature that marked out the great from the merely good in canal building. These were qualities Brindley held in abundance. He seemed to relish fresh challenges and would delight in developing solutions that killed simultaneous birds with a single stone. Many examples of this have already been described but one more may help to serve for emphasis.

When he needed to build an embankment Brindley devised a special type of boat with a trapdoor in its base. Where soil needed to be extracted to build the canal it was loaded into one of these boats and taken to the point where the embankment was being built and the trapdoor opened, thus saving considerable effort with barrows. What was more, when they were no longer needed, these boats could be taken apart and their materials used to construct locks.

During building Brindley would use the canal to help build the canal. He contrived a floating blacksmith's forge, carpenters shop and mason's shop, all floating on behind the work as it progressed. There was even a floating chapel. Elsewhere, Brindley's intuition over-ruled his experience, largely because the problems he encountered were new even to him. The Harecastle Tunnel is a good example of this. Even though tunnels had been built before, never had they been obliged to stay on a single level and proceed in a straight line, regardless of geology.

It is tempting to bestow Brindley with the accolade of brilliance in meeting these challenges, but the truth is probably more prosaic. We have seen that in his early millwrighting work and his dabbling with steam he was an advocate of trial and error, and no doubt there was some of this in his early canal work. As time went on, however, he accumulated a body of experience that was second to none and it is to his credit that he gathered a coterie of apprentices around him to whom he could pass on some of this knowledge.

Perhaps a stronger claim to brilliance lies in Brindley's sheer vision. As we have seen, he did not originate the idea of canals and neither was he the first to appreciate their potential. What he could see, that others couldn't, was how they might be built. He introduced concepts such as aqueducts, embankments and tunnels that seemed preposterous but worked. He could see the big picture not only for individual canals but for the whole system, which he articulated with enviable clarity in his idea of a Grand Cross.

Brindley was a man of his age, an age that predated intellectual specialisation. This was the age of the polyglot, who might practice medicine, be an accomplished musician and dabble in invention. It was an age of ideas, of uncertainties, when new theories could be postulated in geology, astronomy or medicine and discussed without the burden of known laws and proof. It was an age when experimentation could be done in the field (in Brindley's case quite literally), without the need for a laboratory, university or corporate sponsor. Every new discovery only fed the desire for more, every failure sowed the seeds of the need to find answers. It was a unique age, one unrestricted by the need for uniformity and rationality that industrialisation helped to engender.

Canals were perfect for this age. The canal engineer had to be a jack of all trades, capable of supervising the building of bridges, culverts, wharves, warehouses, lock cottages, aqueducts and tunnels – even hedges and fencing. The canals themselves were about more than puddled clay, as any casual observation will show, although the sheer logistics of moving tons of clay should not be underestimated. They were often lined with stone along the edges or reinforced by bricks that were formed and fired *in situ*.

Furthermore, James Brindley, the man, was perfect for canals. His lack of formal education kept his mind open to free thinking. Unencumbered by the prevailing orthodoxy he trusted what his eyes told him worked and he was happy to learn by his mistakes.

Engineering as we understand it today did not exist as a profession in the mid-eighteenth century and Brindley, along with a band of like-minded colleagues such Watt and Stephenson, helped to invent it. Although best remembered for his work with canals, his early work with factories and with steam mark him out as a pioneer. His sheer inventiveness caused him to be consulted on a raft of problems ranging from how to drain the lowlands in Lincolnshire to how to clear Liverpool Docks of mud. He is also credited with creating a way of building sea walls without using mortar.

Like the Human Genome Project in modern times it is probably iniquitous to credit one individual with the invention of a science. In truth, engineering was a science in progression. Blacksmiths had become wrights, and wrights were becoming engineers. Brindley and his associates were on the crest of this change. That Brindley subsequently failed to gain a place in the first division of this group can probably be put down in part to the fate of canals.

However impressive the engineering that created them, it wasn't long before canals were superseded by the far sexier technologies of steam and then the railways. These reached their heyday at the time when engineering's history books were being written and its heroes enshrined. The Institute of Civil Engineering wasn't founded until 1828 and by then canals were rapidly becoming yesterday's thing. As if to illustrate how thin the line between fame and relative obscurity can be, Brindley was known to work with his much more famous contemporary, James Watt, when both were working on the Forth & Clyde Canal. Very similar men with similar interests – canals, steam – it is just that fate sent the two men in different directions. The rest, as they say, is history.

If Newton rationalised his genius as standing on the shoulders of giants, then Brindley's claim is, if anything, stronger, for he was an absolute pioneer in his field. Although canals existed in Europe, Brindley would not have had access to any written details of how they were built and even if he had he wouldn't have understood them. Equally, if Einstein defined genius as one per cent inspiration and ninety-nine per cent perspiration, then again Brindley's claim is a good one, as the ability to deliver pure insight out of the blue was one he demonstrated time and time again. That these qualities were tempered by personality flaws is probably more an illustration of the frustration he felt at constantly being the only one with a clear idea of what was needed than a disqualification for genius.

The deciders in this debate begin with Brindley's sheer breadth of vision and how he combined this with the ability to carry it through. Plenty of people have big ideas; very few bring them to fruition. Add to this his ability to challenge existing orthodoxies and his annoyingly constant habit of being right and the case for greatness has probably been made. Compound this with the impact of his achievements, which will be discussed in greater detail later, and the clincher is that he did what no other person had ever dared or even dreamed to do before. For this author at least this combination of qualities mark him out as a genius.

ten

Harassed on Every Side

As early as 1767 concerns were growing for Brindley's well-being. During March of that year Josiah Wedgwood wrote: 'I am afraid he will do too much and leave us before his vast designs are executed, he is so incessantly harassed on every side, that he hath no rest either for mind or body, and will not be prevailed upon to take proper care of his health.' It is not difficult to find the source of these concerns. Not only was Brindley starting out on his epic tunnel at Harecastle but he was also in much demand from other canal entrepreneurs for surveys, and once these were complete, to act as engineer.

In truth, by this time Pandora's box had been well and truly opened. Everyone wanted a slice of canals and, in lieu of any serious alternative, that meant a slice of Brindley. Now over fifty, Brindley was finding it hard to keep juggling an ever increasing number of balls in the air. Two years into marriage and a new house, he had extended his responsibilities yet further in both his private and his professional life. Against this background it is hardly surprising that he found himself feeling more and more tired, and it is equally reasonable to see how he probably put this down to over-work.

In fact a more sinister force was at work. James Brindley had contracted diabetes, probably what we would today call 'type 2 diabetes'. Formerly called 'maturity diabetes' because it usually appears in middle-aged or elderly people, the symptoms are often confused with simply 'getting older' and therefore explained away. These include feeling tired, going to the toilet more often and blurred vision. It often affects those who are overweight and is caused by the body no longer responding to its own insulin. Tiredness was certainly a problem for Brindley and although he and Anne would regularly make plans for short breaks together, to Scotland, or to Buxton for the waters, these just as often were cancelled at the last minute as a problem only he could solve came up.

When he had been working for the Duke, other than the occasional trip to London, Brindley had been confined to a relatively tight orbit. Now, late in life, he found himself travelling the length and breadth of the country, ironically subjecting himself to the hardships of the turnpike system his canals were soon going to rival. Travelling around the country on

Ayhno Wharf of the Oxford Canal is a typical example of how an original unloading wharf has been converted to modern use.

his horse he was punishing his body with irregular nights and inn food of varying quality, as well as exposing himself daily to whatever the elements chose to throw at him. From enjoying the convivial company of the Duke and staying at Worsley Hall of an evening he was thrown into a situation where he rarely saw his wife and home. A physician could hardly have prescribed a worse regime.

The problem was, and Brindley would have been aware of this, he was really the only man around with the credibility to get a canal scheme off the ground. Although handsome sums were dangled before him to get involved with different schemes it wasn't really the money that made him accept, it was more a sense of responsibility that really, only he could do the job.

This was of course only partially true, and in practice even when he agreed to become the surveyor or engineer to a canal scheme he was only physically able to give a small proportion of his time to it, becoming more of what we would regard today as a consulting engineer. This was recognised in his contracts, which usually stipulated what proportion of his time each client could expect.

The reality was that canal building was an expensive business often requiring private individuals to put up their own cash. Schemes were sold more on the basis of ideas and potential than proven track record. Canals were an unproven investment. Although there could be no such thing as a guarantee, having Brindley's name associated with a scheme was as close as you could get. Without it any new canal proposal stood little chance of progressing.

We can only speculate on Brindley's mental state at this time. A very private man, he had suddenly become public property. Exhausted, removed from his home life and having to manage a harangue of calls on his time, he continued at an almost demonic pace. Although he did turn jobs down, he accepted more than was good for him, finding them hard to refuse if they represented a challenge (including non-canal work) and especially hard to refuse if they furthered or reinforced his vision for a Grand Cross straddling the country. It must also have been quite flattering to be recognised as the country's leading expert in a new and exciting science.

That this pace was unsustainable was clear to Brindley's nearest and dearest yet still he chose to pursue it. He didn't need the money and he had surely won the intellectual argument over the merits of canals and his skills in constructing them, if not the nation's heart. Given that he had a comfortable alternative available to him, why did he continue at this manic rate? It is tempting to speculate that Brindley knew that the clock was ticking against him and he was keen to secure his vision in the time he had left available. There is no evidence for this. His diabetes had not been formally diagnosed, but the physical symptoms of it would have been undeniable, and as we have seen, as early as five years before his death there were concerns that he was living on borrowed time.

Despite his hard fought and largely victorious battles with detractors it is also possible that Brindley was not convinced that he had won the arguments over the superiority of canals, or even if he had that others had yet fully accepted his vision of what form they should take. The technology was still in an early stage and he may well have discerned that plenty of scope remained for men less skilled than himself to hijack his ideas – both on how canals should be built and the configuration they should eventually take.

What Brindley was probably trying to ensure was a momentum capable of outliving him. Even taking into account his perpetual optimism on the time it took to construct a canal it wouldn't have taken much prescience to appreciate that he was never going to live to see a completed system. It was to be his fate to attend a number of opening ceremonies in his time but very few completion parties. With a bit of luck, though, he probably calculated that he might be granted enough time to establish the foundations of a system to his satisfaction. Throughout his career Brindley had always had very clear ideas about the right and the wrong way to do things, the right way almost without exception being his way. This need to establish his hallmark upon the developing system would therefore have been a strong motivator – strong enough to make him deaf to the entreaties of others.

Besides, his involvement in the various schemes he put his name to was often at arms length, with a pattern emerging of him putting associates in place to do the actual surveying under his, often remote, guidance. Indeed, his plans were regularly reinterpreted to such an extent that the eventual canal could hardly be described as one of 'his' at all. That said, he kept in regular touch with the various schemes he was involved with through correspondence, often being called upon to arbitrate on quite minor matters raised by his various clerks of works. Perhaps as a measure of this growing burden his wife Anne began to take on some of the responsibility for this correspondence, and with it a deeper insight into his predicament.

A counter to this argument might be a simpler explanation – that Brindley simply couldn't resist a challenge. The more successful he became the more challenges were directed towards him and once they had fired his imagination he found them difficult to turn away. Today he might be regarded as a workaholic, but the reality was he knew no other way of spending his time.

The actual construction work associated with canal building was largely achieved through sub-contracting different tasks to specialists. As with today, tenders would be issued for elements of the work from the supply of wood to excavation. On the Oxford Canal, for example, records survive that show a contract for cutting the three miles south of the junction with the Coventry Canal. The price to be paid was £350 a mile with extra allowed for cuttings deeper than four feet four inches and embankments higher than three feet. Bridges were an extra £120 each. Elsewhere charges could be set for digging by the cubic yard or yard of progress. These prices excluded all the other associated costs, including the purchase of land and other overheads, which could often bring the tally per mile to anywhere between £2,000 and £4,000.

All this activity was not the canal mania that would invigorate the country and its economy at the end of the century, but it was a good prelude to it. The high watermark of this mania occurred a full twenty years after Brindley's death when eighteen separate Canal Acts were put forward to Parliament in a single year. Nevertheless, the rate at which Brindley picked up fresh commissions during this period was almost embarrassing, especially given his outstanding commitments to the Trent & Mersey and Staffordshire & Worcester Canals.

He had already surveyed a proposed Huddersfield broad canal in 1766 and the following year he was involved with surveys for canals at Bradford in Yorkshire, Rochdale in Lancashire (which would effectively extend the Bridgewater Canal on past Manchester) and Stockton & Darlington in County Durham. Although the last of these was never built, ironically these two towns were the first to be linked by a railway, thus heralding the beginning of the end for canals.

In March 1768 he was appointed Engineer and Surveyor of the proposed Birmingham Canal at a salary of £200 year, in addition to which he was paid £120 for expenses incurred so far by him and his clerk Robert Whitworth, based in London. In September of the same year he accepted the post of Inspector of Works for the Droitwich Canal.

This was a relatively modest canal of only six miles designed to carry coal and salt down into Bristol via the River Severn, but nevertheless brought in a salary of £60 year. In reality, Droitwich presented little challenge to Brindley the engineer, its route following the River Salwarpe to the Severn was self-evident and there was no need for aqueducts and only eight straightforward locks. Nevertheless, it was to Brindley that the financiers behind the canal turned, as he was really the only credible candidate. Perhaps for Brindley the thought of actually starting and finishing a canal was a tempting one, his involvement something he could 'fit in' to his schedule?

The story of the Birmingham Canal is a salutary one. The plan was to link Birmingham with the Staffordshire & Worcester Canal via Wolverhampton and Smethwick. Although only twenty-four miles, this would link the growing city of Birmingham to the nascent system and pass through the valuable coal fields of the Black Country on the way.

Amongst the canal's supporters were Matthew Boulton and Josiah Wedgwood, members of the Lunar Club glitterati of intellectuals, industrialists and entrepreneurs. Brindley's original idea was to replicate the intent of Harecastle by building a tunnel at the canal's summit. Following his death his successors overturned this scheme in favour of locks, which they felt would be cheaper. This they did, but found to their cost that Brindley had been right all along and ended up having to dig a tunnel anyway, incurring an extra expense of £30,000.

This whole episode demonstrates neatly just how far ahead Brindley was of his colleagues, and even though he tried valiantly to pass on his knowledge there really was no substitute for experience and gut feel. Further evidence for Brindley's pre-eminence can be found in the number of occasions that he was asked to pass comment on the plans of other engineers. These included projected improvements to the Thames between London and Reading, the Lancaster, Andover and Salisbury, and Southampton Canals and, in 1768, the Forth & Clyde Canal, a commission that necessitated a trip to Scotland and was combined with a survey of Glasgow Harbour for good measure.

As the Victorian biographer Smiles observed: 'there was scarcely a design of canal navigation set on foot throughout the kingdom during the later years of his life on which he was not consulted and the plans of which he did not entirely make, revise or improve'. That Brindley could apply his natural talent to interpret geologies and topographies covering the spectrum the country could offer is further to his credit.

Detailed accounts of Brindley's involvement in these canals are available in some of the more technical accounts of his life. The most important of them from Brindley's point of view were the proposed Coventry and Oxford canals, which together would form the vital missing southern leg of his Grand Cross. Early on the decision was made to divide responsibility for the northern and southern sections of this stretch between the two companies and almost from day one rivalries emerged and relations between them soured. Today a permanent reminder exists of just how bad things got in the mile-long stretch where the two canals run in parallel near their junction at Hawkesbury, the result of a bitter disagreement over where the two canals should meet.

The Droitwich, seen here at the point at which it joins the Severn, was one of the few Brindley canals to be completed in his lifetime. Today it is sadly dilapidated but there are plans to bring it back to life.

One of the locks on the Droitwich today – still recognisable as a lock but a long way from being serviceable.

As we have already seen, Brindley became involved first with the Coventry Canal, taking a salary of £150 year, for which he undertook to give two months a year of his time. Work on this canal started in earnest early in 1769 but the management committee must have been either particularly awkward or arrogant because Brindley soon found himself at odds with them. Half the committee were aldermen or councillors of the City of Coventry and it seems that their standards were lower than Brindley was prepared to tolerate. They wanted their canal on the cheap.

Before the year was out Brindley experienced that rarity in his career: a dismissal. If anything, however, this served to boost his reputation, for although building continued for another couple of years the canal stalled at Atherstone, sixteen miles out from Coventry and some way from the proposed junction at Fradley. For years this rump of a canal was to exist in isolation, although fortunately for the shareholders it linked the Warwickshire coalfield with Coventry, Nuneaton and Atherstone, thus making this orphaned canal financially viable. The message however was clear: mess with the great man at your peril.

Brindley had also taken responsibility for the survey of the Oxford leg, and having piloted the necessary legislation through Parliament took on the role of Engineer at £200 year. Although Brindley's signature appears on the minutes of a meeting of the committee in May 1772 this was only a few months before his death and it is likely that he only had a passing involvement in the day-to-day planning of the canal once it was underway.

The frustration felt by the canal's committee over an early lack of progress has already been remarked upon, but was not without cause. Brindley had delegated much of the day-to-day work to his assistant Samuel Simcock. Like the Coventry Canal, this leg was inadequately

Brindley's name can just be made out on his grave.

Brindley is buried in a plot next to Jane, Hugh Henshall's wife.

funded and Simcock soon found himself having to respond to demands for economies. His response was to add to the length of the canal with the aim of avoiding expensive cuttings and embankments. In this way the long-term aim of the canal, to create an efficient link between Oxford (and by implication London via the Thames) and the rest of the system, was sacrificed to the short-term expedient of saving money.

In the end the canal's money troubles proved almost terminal and it was forced to pause at Banbury for seven years. As has already been mentioned however, the stretch linking Banbury and Braunston is perhaps the most Brindley-esque on the system. Undulating contours forced Brindley to twist and turn his canal so that it almost tied itself into knots – anything, it seemed, to avoid the need for a lock.

The most infamous example of this is at Wormleighton Hill, where the canal takes a one-mile detour around Wormleighton Manor. Although this can be put down to a desire to avoid locks, the real reason behind this particular convolution is more prosaic. The actual rise involved is not that great, the reason the canal twists so is that the owners of the manor only allowed the canal to cut across their land at all on the condition that there wasn't a lock, as they felt the required pause would prove too great a temptation to boatmen to snaffle the occasional rabbit or pheasant for their pot.

In the end it took twenty-one years to complete the canal, although when it did finally get going again the last stretch from Banbury to Oxford was relatively straightforward, as once again Brindley had chosen a river valley, that of the Cherwell, to follow. The canal actually connects with the Thames in two places, at its terminus and at Wolvercote, where the Duke of Marlborough negotiated a shortcut to the river to service his nearby paper mills. To this day this stretch with its single lock is known as the Duke's Cut.

As the new commissions came forward a pattern began to emerge: of canals linking up coal fields and other sources of mineral wealth, where the bulk transport advantages of waterways came into their own, and of these in turn joining up with each other. The system was beginning to take on the appearance of a shattered windscreen with splinters radiating out from Stoke, Birmingham and Manchester. As this process gathered momentum so the canals added value to each other, creating a virtuous cycle of growth and profit.

Although the ideal was that canals should be linked into other canals, Brindley was not averse to advising on links into river navigations if this was what was required. He was not totally prejudiced against rivers, as his work on the Droitwich Canal and its link into the Severn had proved! Another good example was the Chesterfield Canal, which was started in 1771 with the intention of ferrying coal lime and lead from Derbyshire to the River Trent.

Forty-six miles long, including a significant tunnel 2,880 yards long (exactly the same as the Harecastle), this stand-alone canal, completed after Brindley's death by Hugh Henshall, was highly profitable, proving that you didn't have to connect to the main system in order to succeed. Even today the twenty-six miles to Worksop remain navigable, the tunnel having fallen victim to maintenance costs at the beginning of the last century. The Chesterfield Canal is also tangible proof that Brindley could 'do' locks if required. Perhaps the most spectacular feature of this canal now that its tunnel has gone is the fifteen-lock Thorpe Locks flight with its two- and three-rise staircase locks, which are known to be Brindley's handiwork.

There is a danger that the list of Brindley's growing commitments at this time have come to overshadow his achievements on what was still his main project: the Trent & Mersey Canal, not least his work to carry the canal over the River Dove in Staffordshire. Specifically, this required the building of a series of aqueducts, the longest of which at Clay Cross had twelve sturdy arches.

Aqueducts had by this time become something of a specialist construction for Brindley, whose technique was to dig out banks that were double the width of the river and to build half the structure on dry land. The river could then be diverted to flow beneath these arches and allow Brindley to build the other half, again on dry land, before reverting the river to its original flow. By using this approach Brindley was able to create extra space for flooding and thereby ensure that the contagion of river water would be kept forever away from the purity of his canal.

The sheer logistical exercise that this would have represented, accomplished as it would have been mainly through sweat and muscle, would have been considerable. Brindley took the opportunity of such projects to gather his growing band of acolytes around him to learn his trade and in time these became known as 'the Staffordshire School'. Increasingly, Brindley's way of doing things became the accepted way that things were done, no doubt much to his satisfaction.

The classic example of this is the Brindley Bridge, which has become a feature of much of the English countryside. It is difficult now to envisage that before Brindley swing bridges were the norm. Built either of stone or brick, the gentle arch of the Brindley Bridge, and the oval that is described when it is reflected on still water, evokes qualities of balance and calm, of a natural order, that summarise the essence of canals. So much so indeed that a Brindley Bridge, flanked by bullrushes on one side, is today the logo of British Waterways.

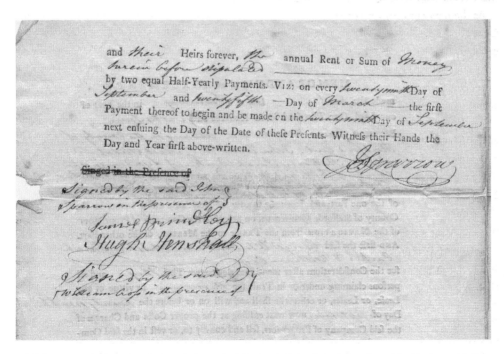

Despite the claims made by some, Brindley was far from illiterate, as this example of his signature amply demonstrates. (Courtesy of The Waterways Archive)

The Napton Flight of locks on the South Oxford Canal leads to a long sweep around the base of the hill topped by a windmill – one of many long sweeps on this typically Brindley-esque canal.

Stalactites inside Brindley's Harecastle Tunnel give the appearance of a gaping shark's mouth. (Courtesy of Dave Lane)

Even at this late stage in his career Brindley was not afraid to be bold, indeed circumstances often demanded it, and his willingness to do things his contemporaries wouldn't touch was part of his attraction. On more than one occasion he would suggest the development of aqueducts, embankments or tunnelling that most of his contemporaries would have balked at, not for effect but in order to maintain his sacred principles of flat water.

During this period Brindley was also called in to help with the proposed Leeds & Liverpool Canal. Like the Trent & Mersey this was an idea that had been around for some time, and a survey had already been completed, although its results had not been satisfactory for its backers. Like many of the schemes he was becoming involved in, what his clients required was an opinion on the work of rival engineers. Once again, as was becoming a trend, Brindley was being asked to act in the role of consulting engineer. Often brought in to give an opinion, more than once he ended up taking on much more.

The Leeds & Liverpool was a daring project: a broad canal capable of taking barges twelve feet wide. When completed it would provide a transport hub for the whole of the Yorkshire and Lancashire manufacturing belt. Brindley was asked to re-survey part of the route, although it is likely that much of the work was in fact carried out by his assistant Robert Whitworth, on whom he was becoming increasingly reliant.

On completion of the survey Brindley reported to two separate meetings, one held in Bradford on the 5 December 1768 and the other in Liverpool four days later, that he estimated that the canal would cost a little over a quarter of a million pounds to construct. When finished it would be 108 miles long and forty-two feet wide with an average depth of five feet.

As an example of the level of financial sophistication of these studies he suggested that the annual running costs of the canal would be £17,000, comprised of £13,000 in interest at five per cent a year and the rest as expenses and salaries, suggesting a low level of necessary maintenance. Against this could be offset income at £20,000 a year. £8,500 of this would come from the transport of limestone, lime, slate, flags, brick and freestone at a halfpenny per ton/mile. £3,500 would come from the transport of coal at a penny a ton/mile and the remainder from the carriage of lead, timber, textiles, cutlery(!) and groceries at one and a half pence a ton/mile. Not bad for a supposed illiterate.

To a modern accountant this would represent a very modest return and indeed a fragile level of viability, but it seemed to be enough as the canal was given the go ahead anyway, suggesting that Brindley could probably have said anything reasonable and it would have been accepted. Once the canal gained its Parliamentary Assent the Directors of the company duly offered him the role of Engineer but Brindley felt obliged to turn this one down. Even he had to admit that he simply had too much on. Besides, the Leeds & Liverpool would be a tributary to, rather than a component part of, the Grand Cross. Brindley would have been heartily in favour of it as an example of the value canals could add to each other, but it would not have been one of his primary concerns.

Even taking into account the already remarked upon tendency of contemporary commentators towards hyperbole, the following account of his endeavours at this time, published in 1769 in *A History of Inland Navigations* paints a powerful picture both of Brindley's standing at that time and his continuing achievements:

> *'[Mr Brindley], great in himself, harbours no contracted notions, no jealousy of rivals; he conceals not his methods of proceeding nor asks patents to secure the sole use of the machines which he*

invents and exposes to public view: sensible that he must one day cease to be, he selects men of genius, teaches them the power of mechanics and employs them in carrying on the various undertakings in which he is engaged … He is of public utility and employs his talents in rectifying the mistakes of despairing workmen and in setting on foot large and useful machines in the silk throwing, mill working, mine draining and various other ways, by which he opens new veins of treasure to Great Britain.'

Although he was the country's leading canal guru, Brindley was not omnipotent. His preference for canals over rivers was well known, but not even Brindley could argue the case for canals over Old Father Thames. In 1770 he was employed by the Corporation of London to advise how best to improve the navigation of the Thames above Battersea. Brindley's response was nothing if not predictable – why not build a canal instead? As well as the usual concerns about tides, floods and silt, Brindley argued that a canal would be both cheaper and quicker. Cheaper and quicker or not, the Corporation had nothing to do with this plan and it was quickly dropped.

Brindley, it seemed, had not won over the more conservative-minded and refined sensibilities of the London establishment. It seems that up to and even after his death he remained in their eyes something of a coarse-speaking provincial upstart. His achievements in what they would have regarded as the industrial backwaters of the north would have been of passing interest, but not something they would have wanted to get involved in. The Victorian biographer Smiles makes the valid point that Brindley's contemporary, the diarist and traveller Samuel Johnson, never mentioned canals in any of his works, despite the fact that his frequent trips to his home county of Staffordshire would have cast the raw evidence of their existence sharply into his consciousness.

Evidence of Brindley having over-stretched himself echoes through the chronicle of his last few years. It wasn't only the Oxford Canal Committee that had cause to bemoan his almost total absence but the Birmingham Canal also complained that they never saw him, or that when he did deign to visit he didn't take time to report to the Committee. Whilst Anne might be able to keep the various committees at bay, it was beyond the physical capability of one man to cope with the growing administrative burden being placed upon him. Brindley's temper, always slumbering beneath the surface, would occasionally erupt, fired no doubt by a dangerous cocktail of stress, overwork and tiredness made worse by his condition.

Brindley was happiest when he was out in the open air planning or executing a canal. When the Management Committee of the Trent and Mersey Canal decided that they wanted to cut a branch line off the summit at Etruria to Froghall near Leek in order to create access to the limestone at Caldon Low, Brindley must have jumped at the chance to survey the route. For him this was home turf, not only could he metaphorically get his hands dirty but there was even a chance that he might occasionally get to sleep in his own bed. Finally, this was land he knew well. No long horse journeys or surveys of foreign soil and topography, no accents he had to struggle to understand from the locals. With hindsight, the decision to accept the commission was loaded with irony.

In September 1772 Brindley was close to finishing his survey when he was caught in a shower of rain that saturated both his clothes and his skin. Given his frequent exposure to the elements this wasn't an unusual occurrence but it hit him hard so he was taken to an inn in the

One of the trademarks of Brindley's South Oxford Canal, a lifting bridge.

nearby village of Ipstones, about ten miles away from Turnhurst. Unfortunately, the innkeeper didn't maintain the highest of hotel standards and the bed he was placed in was damp, causing what had started as a chill to develop into something altogether more serious.

It became clear fairly soon that Brindley's illness had established a grip and he was taken home. Erasmus Darwin visited and was the first to finally diagnose the malady that had been troubling Brindley for some time, his diabetes. It was all too late, there was little anyone could do but nurse him. Slowly, but inexorably, Brindley began to slip away; but there was still time for him to experience further harassment from those who had demanded his attention over the last few years and driven him to the state he was now in.

A delegation appeared demanding advice on some canal works. Incredibly, Brindley granted them an audience and when told that they were experiencing problems with leakage advised them to puddle the banks. When his supplicants explained that they had already done this Brindley unleashed his acid tongue, telling them to 'puddle it again and again'. Even on his deathbed, it seemed, he was indispensable.

His old friend Josiah Wedgwood visited and stayed, but knew what was coming. Together with Anne he kept a vigil. Around noon on 27 September 1772 Wedgwood dabbed some of his beloved water on his lips and Brindley brushed him aside saying simply and prophetically 'It's enough, I shall need no more'. With that, according to Wedgwood, he shut his eyes, never to open them again.

* * * * * * * * * *

A rare example of a straight stretch on a Brindley canal, although appearances can be deceptive as this run at Fenny Compton on the South Oxford Canal was in fact once a tunnel and has since been opened out.

James Brindley was buried at his local church in Newchapel. An unostentatious rectangular building of red brick with a small copper-clad spire and a tiled roof, the church sits on a hill and looks down on the site where Turnhurst lay until its demolition in 1929. Today the view is of Staffordshire farmland, large proportions of which have been converted into a golf course or sold off for modern housing. Adjacent to Brindley's modest grave lie those of the Henshall family, including his loyal assistant Hugh, and members of the Williamson family. Initially the graves were surrounded by metal railings, but these were removed when the graves were restored and relocated in 1956.

Hugh proved to be a big help to Anne in the weeks and months immediately after her husband's death. Although Brindley had died a wealthy man his estate took some time to unravel and for months after his death Anne had to chase money owing to him. There was also the small matter of achieving probate on Brindley's father's will, following his death two years before, something he had never quite got round to doing himself as he had been too busy. Hugh also responded by taking up the flame of Brindley's cause, not only writing a glowing obituary of him but also taking over as Chief Engineer on many of the canal projects Brindley had committed himself to.

Three years after Brindley's death Anne remarried, becoming the bride of Robert Williamson and mother to seven of his children, in addition to the two daughters she bore Brindley in the last two years of his life. Anne lived a full life and died a day before the fifty-fourth anniversary of her first husband's demise. Her eldest daughter Ann never married and died at sea returning from Australia.

Her second daughter, Susannah, did marry and bore two sons. Brindley would hardly have known this daughter as she was born the year he died, but his memory and achievements were clearly kept alive in her as she chose to name her firstborn James Brindley Bettingdon and her second John Henshall Bettingdon. Sadly, Susannah herself died when only twenty-seven, two weeks after Anne's second husband went, leaving her a widow once again.

In the late 1950s a descendant of the elder grandson described the meagre possessions of his namesake still in the family's possession. These included a lock of greying hair, the miniature portrait described earlier, a seal, a ticket conferring the title of Burgess on him from the City of Glasgow and the Bible given to him by the Duke of Bridgewater. Apart from the theodolite at the Brindley Mill and his journals these are all that remains.

All that is apart from his canals. James Brindley did what few of us manage – he left an indelible mark upon the countryside of his homeland. In a dozen short years he had an involvement in the development of 350 miles of canals, forming the framework from which an entire system sprang. May 1772 saw the opening of the Staffordshire and Worcester Canal. Although the Trent and Mersey had yet to be completed the stretch linking the Trent with Stoke was finished. Consequently, the first axis of Brindley's Grand Cross, linking Hull with Bristol, was complete and Brindley had just lived to see it.

The importance of this canal has often been under-estimated by historians. By opening up the coalfields of Wolverhampton it acted as the catalyst for a range of iron-working industries that themselves formed an exemplar for the industrial revolution that followed. What was more, output from these industries, and from Wedgwood's factories, could be exported to the colonies and Europe. Raw materials from other parts of the country as well as abroad, along with goods and basics such as food, could be imported into the landlocked heart of the country, feeding both people and invention.

On completion, the Staffordshire and Worcester joined the elite club of Brindley canals that were finished in their master's lifetime. Others included the Bridgewater, of course, the short Droitwich and, by only a week, the Birmingham. But Brindley had done just enough to make sure that the canals he started could continue and didn't simply expire with him. A momentum had been created along with a sufficient body of skills and knowledge to take the dream forward. It is true that some of the canals he left behind stuttered after his death, but in time they nearly all made it.

By the time the Oxford Canal was completed, and the Grand Cross was finally realised in 1790, the stage was set for a spate of activity no one in England, Europe or the world had ever seen before. As with the 'dot-com' boom of the late 1990s, anyone with a half-decent plan with the word 'canal' in it could get backing. Some were built but many ended up as ugly incomplete gashes on the landscape. Although many investors got hurt, some got very rich indeed and the net result was a realignment of the transport network.

Many of the new canals were built to repair the impact of the 'four-mile rule' agreed to by the early pioneers in order to appease the turnpikes and other vested interests. Under this rule the pioneers had agreed that no new canal should pass within four miles of a town. Whilst the Grand Cross provided the main motorways of the system it soon became clear that what was really needed was a network of A and B roads to feed into it. Branch lines proliferated to such an extent that even today half the population live within five miles of a canal.

It is clear that the technology and demand were in place to allow the canals to be built. Complementing these were the social and economic conditions to support them. What is less clear is whether these would have been enough on their own or whether it took a Brindley to make them happen. In order to decide whether Brindley truly was the man who united the kingdom we need an answer to this question and an assessment of his true impact and legacy.

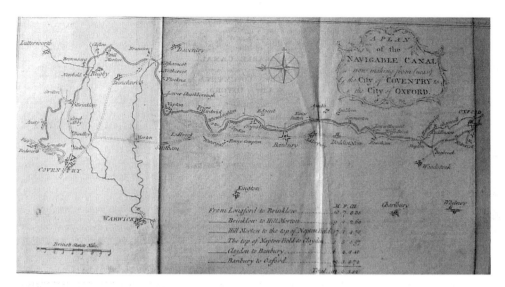

Canal plans were often rudimentary – a statement of intent rather than a working plan, as this map stating the route of the Oxford Canal shows. (Courtesy of The Waterways Archive)

eleven

Of Public Utility

A Barton Aqueduct survives to this day, but it is not Brindley's masterpiece. Instead a swing bridge, equally remarkable in its time, has taken its place. A latticework box of grey steel and sharp edges, it cradles and channels the dark still water of the canal in its hand. Traffic these days is light but steady, but there are no horses and no sailing craft, their relative silence has been replaced by the steady chugging of diesel engines powering leisure craft.

Opinion is divided as to the aesthetic merit of the new bridge, but there's something about it that is very Cubist and at the same time very Tate Modern, a reminder perhaps that views on what constitutes beauty come and go. Its single most distinguishing feature is the fact that it can be sealed at each end and its 1450 tons, including 800 tons of water, can be pivoted about the middle. In many ways it is a fitting tribute to Brindley, not least because it was an example of cutting edge engineering when it was built in the late 1890s.

The new bridge is wide enough to take two boats and when it swings open it is a sight worth seeing as the canal defers to the superior forces that usurped it by pivoting on a small brick plinth. Below the bridge two deep cliffs line straight, parallel banks stretching either side that disappear into their respective vanishing points. Ironically, perhaps, the men in charge of the Irwell eventually won the battle for supremacy, but to achieve it they had to transform their river into another canal, the Manchester Ship Canal, so victory came at a high price.

Brindley's magnificent structure became an obstacle to the progress of the large ocean-going craft making their way to Salford Docks and had to go. Brindley had the last laugh, however. Even with the benefit of explosives the demolition men had tremendous problems dislodging the aqueduct's pilings. Brindley had used massive two-foot square timbers and enclosed them in clay. Protected from the water they had hardly rotted at all and proved a formidable obstacle. As a consequence England's first major canal was effectively supplanted by its last. Although the Bridgewater remains it is owned today by its much larger rival. Brindley's structure stood for 130 years, a period that spanned from the beginning to the end of canals as a viable commercial proposition.

The impact of canals even in Brindley's time was immediate and dramatic, both on individual localities and, in a deeper psychological sense, on the nation as a whole. In the period immediately after his death they cemented this impact and weaved their way into the fabric of the nation, physically and emotionally.

The first and most visible evidence of the impact a canal could have was seen in Manchester. True to his word, the Duke's canal cut the price of coal in half instantly. Not only did this have a direct impact upon the comfort of the local population but, at least as important, they were assured of a regular supply. The cycle of feast and famine, for food as well as fuel, was broken. By happy coincidence the new steam engines also required coal, and with reliable supplies assured local entrepreneurs could invest in industry with confidence.

Within half a generation the industrial landscape of Manchester was transformed. Pastures and ponds were replaced by a busy combination of factories, warehouses, shipyards, corn silos and, most importantly, cotton works. Great sheets of cotton dominated the skyline, drying in Manchester's ample winds, fresh dyes offering a kaleidoscope of colour. Capitalism's virtuous cycle was initiated. Investment led to jobs, which in turn created demand and greater diversity. A hot bed of markets and consumerism was born. Soon the small houses, narrow streets and air of menace that had become Manchester's trademark were replaced by daring new buildings, a hubbub of activity and a climate of confidence. Poverty remained, of course, but this was a town on the rise, and rapidly so.

The photograph of Brindley's aqueduct just before it was demolished gives a sense of its solid construction. (Courtesy of The Waterways Archive)

When it came, access to Liverpool meant access to foreign markets. Cottons previously hauled on the backs of reluctant donkeys and horses to Bewdley or Bridgenorth on the Severn were immediately diverted to the Mersey. With the rapidity enjoyed by Manchester, Liverpool became a different place, soon usurping Bristol as the most important port on the west coast. The absence of canals meant that the south-western part of the country, no less blessed with raw materials than the north, had to wait before it could exploit its economic potential.

Critically, by linking the two great centres of population in the north west the Bridgewater Canal provided a spindle around which the whole region could rotate. A whole list of towns including Bolton, Burnley and Rochdale could experience the Manchester effect. When the Leeds and Liverpool Canal opened these were joined by others across the Pennines. The economy had found a new foundation, one that not even London could afford to ignore, leading in turn to pressures for wider political and social reform.

Canals also lived up to all their promise for other areas such as the Potteries and the Black Country. Within the country previously unconnected areas discovered a new inter-dependency. Salt mined in Cheshire was distributed throughout the country. Cornish clay was brought in direct to the Potteries, likewise gypsum from Northwich. From being an ill-organised collection of skills and cottage-based industries, the Potteries trebled in size before the end of the century and the industry there achieved a critical mass. At the same time the country gained a truly national economy.

The same was true for the export trade. Even before the Trent and Mersey Canal opened, upwards of £100,000 worth of pottery was already being exported from Burslem every year. After the canal was opened this figure grew exponentially. Markets in the colonies in North America were a particular focus for trade from Liverpool, with Wedgwood's pottery a favourite there, then as now. Ale from Burton, already popular in Germany, also found new markets in America, as did the output of the light metal works in the Midlands.

The canals transported timber for houses and brickworks became a popular canalside industry, helping to fuel a radical change in how houses were constructed and in the material comfort of a huge proportion of the population. Mud floors were replaced by tiles. Families ate not off wooden platters but ceramic plates, and pewter mugs were replaced by glass and china. People even gained their own knives and forks, made out of metal no less! Odd items previously regarded as luxuries crept into even the most humble of homes, an iron candlestick perhaps, a china tea or chamber-pot or maybe a mirror. The idea of the impulse buy became possible. Capitalism and consumerism were finding their feet together and feeding off each other.

Even within Brindley's lifetime there had been a radical change in how people lived, clothed and fed themselves. By unblocking the sclerosis of the country's transport arteries the canals gave added momentum to this process. Although the turnpikes continued to spin their web across the country, growing by a third in distance between 1750 and 1770 to a total of 5,000 miles, road transport remained an unpleasant activity, best avoided. They were also expensive and unreliable. Horses pulling over-laden carts would continue to get stuck in muddy ruts from which the only rescue was to put a shoulder to wheels often as tall as the men pushing them. Jams would occur when two such carts approached each other from opposite directions and the byways would be populated by vagrants and rats, both feeding off spilled cargo.

Canals allowed for the bulk transport of raw materials and finished goods. A horse could pull sixty-times more on water than it could on the road and it was in the transfer of goods rather than people that canals scored. That said, people were becoming more mobile, especially when innovations by the likes of Thomas Telford and John MacAdam towards the end of the century improved road surfaces. This increasingly fluid population became free atoms capable of coalescing and being attracted to the new centres of economic activity. The pull of the parish was weakened and with it the influence of the church. People did begin to travel outside an immediate orbit of one day's walk and see how their neighbours lived their lives and compare notes.

Although the country did not modernise in Brindley's day it began the journey to modernisation, a trip that was taken to a considerable extent on the canals. Mass production was still the exception rather than the rule. Most goods were still hand produced in individual cottages and sold at marketplaces. Early factories did exist, not least the silk mills Brindley himself helped to create, and there was one silk mill in Derbyshire that employed 500 people, but it was only partially successful. More practically, the canals made it possible to transport the stone to build such monoliths.

The best examples of mass organisation of labour were probably the naval dockyards, but they had the advantage of enforced discipline, a lesson the coming wave of factory owners were to learn quickly. Manufacturers were still experimenting with the best ways of organising their resources, but they were getting there. A ready availability of fuel, materials and labour made possible largely through the advent of the canals made planning easier, investment less risky and capitalism possible.

At the same time the principle of economy of scale was becoming better understood. Adam Smith in his seminal work *The Wealth of Nations*, published in 1776, spelled out the benefits of the division of labour by using the example of a pin factory. Steam engines meant that the power to drive machinery became less dependent on geography, on access to water or wind. It wouldn't be long before goods became standardised, prices comparable, relative value for money assessable – the basic building blocks of a capitalist economy.

The old ways were still the most trusted ways, but alternatives and change were entering most peoples' lives. In 1751 the country had introduced the Gregorian calendar, an event that had occasioned riots at the perceived theft of eleven days. The canals altered peoples' understanding of change. Previously change had tended to be incremental, an alteration that made the existing way of doing things that bit better. Canals introduced the idea of step change, of a completely new way of doing things.

It was this idea, and the implications of what that change could bring, that was so hard for many to comprehend and led to the initial resistance to canals. Once understood, this appreciation had massive ramifications, not least in the application of steam power that moved from the mines and into the heart of the new industrial towns and brought its own brand of radical change. Economic, and in turn social, revolution was possible through technological innovation and was something that could be embraced rather than fought.

The canals caught the crest of a mood in favour of improvement, experiment and betterment – qualities ably summed up by the Schemer himself, James Brindley. This mood was also illustrated by the founding in 1754 of the Society of Arts, which gave prizes for innovations on the grounds that they were not patented and made available to all, again a sentiment Brindley adhered to. It was suddenly okay for man to take control of his own destiny, to master nature rather than be a slave to it. Even the humblest peasant could begin to think beyond surviving today towards improvement tomorrow. Although probably not conscious at the time, the canals locked into this *Zeitgeist* and gave a tangible representation of it.

Within two decades radical change was indeed becoming the norm as society standardised and normalised, congregating around some kind of sense of common identity and purpose. Ideas of nationhood, often highly abstract before this time as most people associated more with their immediate neighbourhood first, their village or town second and their country a distant third, began to crystallise.

Better communications meant that more people got to know of the triumphs of the army and navy abroad, as well as those of British merchants, and could feel a measure of pride in their country. Previously the nation was present mainly in the monarch, who in turn lived in London, a city so distant for most that it might as well have been Paris or Rome. As the country's dots began to join up ideas of national belonging grew. The nation became 'us' rather than 'them'.

Furthermore, the canals offered a highly practical means of securing the security of the nation. The uprising of 1745 was still livid in many memories. It had been all too easy for the Scottish invaders to wend their way halfway to London before an army could be got up to stop them. With the canals all this changed. As the author of *A History of Inland Navigations* observed: 'In case of invasion or rebellion, by these canals our government would be able to transport their heaviest cannon to any part of the country in a very short time, as also regiments and their baggage could be conveyed in a much faster way than by long tedious harassing marches through roads.'

Innocent to the eye, simple shallow linocut grooves gouged into the soft mud of open fields, the creation of the canals heralded an age when the country lost its rural innocence and its

To this day, boaters can count their progress down the Grand Union Canal using the regular mileposts.

reliance on the seasons. At first they represented a loud imposition on the natural beauty of the countryside with their raw barren edges, unwanted spoil and memories of the vagrants who created them. In time, however, they blended in and became part of the landscape. The economy kicked into gear rather than being constantly kicked out of it by harvest failures and epidemics. The future became something to look forward to rather than something to dread or endure.

In the end the canals had their moment in the sun and were overshadowed by the railways. They fought their corner long and hard but were eventually killed off by the relentless pressure of first the railways, then the internal combustion engine and finally the Great War, which eradicated many of the men and skills needed to keep the system going. One by one the canal companies were bought up by the railways, sometimes because the canals had usurped the most favourable flat route between two places and sometimes simply to buy off the opposition, railway shares being more powerful than canal company shares.

* * * * * * * * * *

Many of the changes canals brought about flowed after Brindley's death and were so multi-faceted and comprehensive in their impact that they can only be fully appreciated with the benefit of hindsight. History is littered with 'might have beens' and it is time to consider whether these changes would have occurred with or without the canals, or indeed whether the canals would have been built if James Brindley hadn't come along?

Prior to the coming of the canals England was an economic boom waiting to happen. Indeed, London was already one of the most prosperous and diverse cities in Europe. A seething cauldron of consumption, London was a beast with an insatiable appetite, able to gobble up whatever was thrown in its direction, be it people or goods. A new technological age had begun to flex its muscles through inventions such as Kay's Flying Shuttle (1733), Arkwright's Water Frame (1769), Crompton's Mule (1779) and of course Watt's separate condenser steam engine patented in 1774.

Equally, England was a mass of communities waiting to be pulled together. Often quite distinct, with their own traditions, dialects, economic specialisations and prejudices, certainly by European standards, England was nevertheless a relatively homogenous society. Although not always comprehensible to outsiders, there was at least a single language, a single law and a single king.

What was lacking in each case was something to bind them together. This is the role that the canals performed. Yes, it probably would have happened anyway, the turnpikes would have eventually become established and improved but, as has already been suggested, it would not have happened as quickly; and by uniting the kingdom so rapidly the canals performed a considerable service to the people, society and economy.

As other countries were soon to discover, the process of industrialisation requires destruction before construction. Old orders, mores and hierarchies have to be challenged and if they won't reform, toppled. In converting from a rural to an urban economy new demands have to be accommodated. The most basic of these is the need to feed huge congregations of people in

The small mouth of the modern Harecastle Tunnel north portal still seems imposing.

a confined space, something the canals made a lot easier. Critically, land has to become more productive and canals, with their boatloads of lime and manure, could oblige.

Perhaps most significant of all in this process is the need to ensure a more even distribution of prosperity and opportunity. Before the canals there was a danger that satisfying the demands of London was set to become the sole purpose of the economy. With their special capacity for bulk transport the canals opened up the new extractive industries of the North, as well as the export-friendly manufacturing of the Midlands, thereby creating not only whole new dimensions to the economy but fresh loci of power.

Prior to the canals the major towns outside London were mainly on the coast. By providing access to the sea for the landlocked potential in the centre of the country this became less of an issue. If the canal system hadn't been built it is likely that the turnpikes would have continued to focus on establishing yet stronger links with London, rather than criss-crossing and uniting the country in the way the Grand Cross achieved.

Once the canal system was established food riots became largely a thing of the past. Rioting still took place – this was by no means a perfect society – but a shortage of food was rarely the cause; rather a fairer distribution of the spoils of prosperity was what would bring people onto the streets. Busy well-fed people who can see a brighter future for themselves and their children need a lot of convincing to riot.

It would be naïve to suggest that all the changes connected with industrialisation were beneficial. Debate on the advantages and disadvantages of the process is as active today as it was when it started and has been amply covered elsewhere. The point is that with the canals the genie was let out of the bottle. Although industrialisation was inevitable, the development of canals sped the whole process up significantly.

In recent years a number of statues and other civic memorials have begun to appear celebrating Brindley, including this one at the entrance to the Caldon Canal in Staffordshire.

Through canals Britain was able to exploit its advantages of relative geographical compactness and an abundance of natural resources much quicker than its economic rivals. As a result the country gained an invaluable head start that subsequent rulers, merchants and chancers were able to exploit for over a century. In many ways, it is possible to assert that Brindley was the man whose work united the kingdom in a real and practical sense.

Canals were not a new idea but critically, Brindley made them happen. Attempts had been made before to harness inland waterways and schemes were being proposed or even attempted contemporaneously to Brindley. As we have seen, the idea of a Trent to Mersey canal predated the Bridgewater, and the potential of a cross-Pennine link was also well understood. The point is, though, that no one had managed to make them happen. Looking back it is easy to suggest that canals were inevitable and Brindley just happened to be in the right place at the right time, but the ability to turn concepts into reality should never be underestimated. It is worth noting that the development of the canal network had a slight stall after Brindley's death, despite his efforts to train a cadre of worthy successors.

Brindley offered that rare combination of grand vision and detailed thinking. If he had a flaw it was in the bridge between the two, dealing with the day-to-day niggles of project management. Give him an engineering problem and the chances were he would solve it. Ask him to manage the men and resources and do it to budget and he would probably let you down. He also possessed a streak of obstinacy that meant that if he felt something was right he would make sure it happened.

Perhaps his real skill was in making it look so easy, especially when one takes into account the lack of precedent. Spice this with the ability to solve problems that stumped his peers and an apparent capacity not to be fazed by the scale of an enterprise and you probably have a combination that was indeed unique – in the sense that if he hadn't been available the whole idea of a comprehensive canal network would never have been realised.

In the context of his day the Bridgewater Canal was a stupendously risky venture. If it had failed, taking a peer of the realm with it, it is likely that it would have been impossible to raise the finance for a second attempt elsewhere. The prospect of failure hovered over the scheme on numerous occasions and on a technological level it is probably fair to say that without Brindley any one of the many obstacles put in its path would have made the difference. If the Duke of Bridgewater is credited with being the father of the canals, then Brindley was the nurse who nourished, nurtured and reared the baby to the point where it was able to fend for itself.

If the Bridgewater had failed then that would probably have put paid to any idea of canals for at least a generation, if not forever. Instead the country would have muddled along on turnpikes and river navigations and that vital kick-start and head start to industrialisation would have been lost. Whilst there may be room for debate over Brindley's greatest achievement – the Barton Aqueduct, the Harecastle Tunnel, the idea of the Grand Cross – there is little doubt that his greatest legacy was the fact that the Bridgewater Canal did not fail, thus paving the way for the maelstrom of activity that followed.

The fact that his legacy has lived on and matured with the times is perhaps the final confirmation of the value of his contribution. Today 2,000 miles of canal remain open, although the emphasis now is on craft not cargo, on leisure not commerce. In an age when spending rather than production is the engine of the economy this is perhaps appropriate.

Even this use of the canals was predicted during Brindley's time, as the following extract in 'A Letter to a Lady' in *A History of Inland Navigations* suggested: 'What a most noble convenience this will be for travellers – we should then travel with as much safety, certainty and despatch as in … Holland or Flanders and in the same manner; for, as here there is no current to impede the vessel, one horse will draw fifty tons of coals after the rate of four miles an hour; and would trot with a light boat and passengers six or seven; and if boats were covered we might travel by night or by day, and sleep, read, write, play at cards, drink tea, and partake of a thousand diversions.'

On today's canals, past and present coexist side by side. The modern boater enjoys the romantic image of slow progress marked only by a gentle wash breaking at the back of their boat. The peace may be disturbed only by the call of a distant warbler, the splash of a tiddler breaking the water's surface or a squawking duckling seeking its mother. At times the whooshing sound of an approaching express or the rattle of a bone-breaking commuter train might break that peace and provide a temporary reminder of the fate of the canals.

At a time when the rail network is in crisis the canals are enjoying a renaissance more miles of waterway are being restored and brought back into service every year than were being built during Brindley's time. There is even talk of cutting brand new canals, and in Scotland the newly opened Falkirk Wheel, with its huge rotary arm transferring boats between different levels like passengers on a Ferris Wheel, is perhaps the modern day equivalent of the Barton Aqueduct. Over 100-feet high, this structure links the Forth and Clyde Canal that Brindley advised upon, with the Union Canal and is capable of carrying the combined weight of 100 elephants, although little demand is expected to prove this. It does so by using the same amount of power as two electric showers.

Elsewhere enough fibre-optic cable has been laid below the system's towpaths for every person in Britain to make a simultaneous phone call, and at a time when the country is affected by periodic droughts, the canal's Watergrid is helping to even out the distribution of this vital resource. Already, canals supply half of Bristol's drinking water. They also provide vital havens for wildlife in places otherwise dominated by concrete.

As for Brindley, the revival of interest in the canals has led to a few more permanent reminders of his achievements popping up. Worsley has made it to a government short list to become a World Heritage Site. A life once marked only by an ash tree at his birthplace is now commemorated through the occasional statue and by naming shopping centres, streets and pubs after him. Brindley Place in the heart of Birmingham is perhaps the most famous of these. At the epicentre of the most complex part of the country's inland waterways system, strings of intricately decorated leisure craft moor up beside the occasional cargo boat selling domestic coal.

This then is the current state of Brindley's legacy. How many of us will be happy if, when we die, we are able to say that we initiated a technological revolution the product of which will be so flexible and durable that it will survive over 200 years?

Yes, Brindley was in the right place at the right time, but having a good idea is never enough on its own. What he gave was vision, guts, intuition and the sheer bloody mindedness to make canals happen. He was given an opportunity and seized it with both hands, literally working himself to death to fulfil it. In an age that relies more on precision, proof and a balanced business plan to advance perhaps there is a lesson here for us all? All non-credited photographs are copyright of the author.

A Note on Sources

As might be expected, most of the primary sources of information about James Brindley have been thoroughly mined over the years and I am indebted to the work of those who have gone before. In writing this book it was not my intention to produce a dry academic treatise on Brindley's life. Instead I wanted to draw upon the excellent work already done, test and expand it with supportive research of my own and offer a fresh assessment of Brindley, his life and legacy. Below I have listed the most prominent of those sources I have used, although this is not by any means a comprehensive list.

Any biographer of Brindley has to be indebted to Samuel Smiles' 1861 biography published in *Lives of the Engineers Vol. 1 (David and Charles)*, although any appreciation of this comprehensive book has to make allowances for the at times fanciful language and uncritical approach taken by the author.

Kathleen Evans' *James Brindley, Canal Engineer – a new Perspective (Churnet Valley Books, 1998)* is particularly authoritative on the Brindley genealogy and the history of some of the canal companies Brindley worked for, whilst Cyril Boucher's *James Brindley Engineer, 1716–1772 (Jarrold and Sons, 1968)* is strong on Brindley's engineering achievements, if a little dependent on Smiles for details on Brindley's life. For those seeking a brief synopsis of Brindley they may wish to refer to Harold Bode's *James Brindley (Shire Books, 1999)*, although inevitably in this short volume analysis is sacrificed on the altar of brevity.

Other invaluable sources include contemporary descriptions in Kippis' *Biographia Britannica (1778–93)*, whose entry on Brindley is generally acknowledged to have been written by Hugh Henshall, and John Philips' *History of Inland Navigations (1805)*. Also worthy of mention is *The Great Duke of Bridgewater* from the wonderfully titled volume *Lancashire Worthies* published in 1874. Other unattributed biographies of Brindley and others of his contemporaries also provide a good insight into how Brindley was perceived shortly after his death.

More general contemporary sources include John Aitkin's *A Description of the Country from Thirty to Forty Miles Around Manchester (1795)* as well as the Manchester Mercury. Amongst numerous specific sources the vitriol of Francis Henry Egerton's *A Letter to the Parisians and the French Nation Upon Inland Navigation* remains fun to read.

Specific modern sources on Brindley and his achievements include Hugh Malet's *The Canal Duke (David and Charles, 1961)* and the same author's pamphlet for the British Waterways Board in the 1980s entitled *Brindley and Canals*, as well as Glen Atkinson's *The Canal Duke's Collieries (1982)*. I would also mention Anthony Burton and Derek Pratt's *The Anatomy of Canals: The Early Years (Tempus Publishing, 2001)* for its insight into the development of the modern canal system. Background research also involved searching a number of websites, too many to detail here, where time and again useful insights and snippets were gained.

Social and economic background was drawn from a variety of sources. Worthy of note are James Woodforde's *The Diary of a Country Parson 1758–1802 (Ed. John Beresford, Oxford University Press, 1978)*, Ray Porter's excellent *English Society in the 18th Century (Penguin, 1990)* and the *Oxford Illustrated History of Britain (Oxford University Press, 1984)*, edited by Kenneth O. Morgan. Finally, a mention for Jenny Uglow's *The Lunar Men: A Story of Science, Art, Invention and Passion (Faber and Faber, 2002)*, which gives a detailed impression of the cauldron of fresh thought going on across all disciplines during Brindley's time.

Finally, this book would not have been possible without the generous assistance of many people. Particularly worthy of mention are the enthusiastic volunteers at the Brindley Mill at Leek, in particular Brian Moran, the expert guidance of the archive and local studies staff at Manchester Central Library and the Waterways Trust in Gloucester, and the archivists at the Institute of Civil Engineers. Thanks are also due to all who freely gave of their time and also to those who gave permission for the use of photographs and images for inclusion in this book.

Index